Dear Friends,

    If you're holding this book in your hands, you've already taken the first step to knowing the unstoppable Gabi Diamond better. Whether you're a fan of the show or just curious how a girl like Gabi manages to juggle it all, the answers to all your questions are right inside. Gabi Moskowitz, whose blog, brokeassgourmet.com, inspired *Young & Hungry*, and Diana Snyder, a writer on our show, have put together advice and recipes for every real-life Gabi and Sofia out there. Maybe you haven't slept with your boss or used a bicycle pump to cook a duck, but almost everyone has forgotten to pay a bill or fallen for someone unobtainable. The things I love most about playing Gabi are her fearlessness, her undeniable spirit, and her positivity. There is no goal she can't achieve, no matter how ridiculous. She's got what it takes, and so do you—because the key to living a young and hungry life is knowing how to feed your soul.

Enjoy!
Emily Osment

# young & HUNGRY

## Your Complete Guide to a Delicious Life

Gabi Moskowitz  Diana Snyder

FREEFORM
Los Angeles · New York

Published by Freeform, an imprint of Disney Book Group. No part of this book may be reproduced or transmitted in any form or by any means, electronic or mechanical, including photocopying, recording, or by any information storage and retrieval system, without written permission from the publisher. Third-party trademarks are indicated by use of an initial capital in their names.

For information address
Freeform, 1101 Flower Street, Glendale, California 91201.

Editor in Chief: Emily Meehan
Executive Editor: Laura Hopper
Design by Julie Rose
Illustrations by Vivien Wu

ISBN 978-1-368-00000-0
FAC-008598-17172

Printed in the United States of America

First Paperback Edition, April 2017

3 5 7 9 10 8 6 4 2

SUSTAINABLE FORESTRY INITIATIVE   Certified Sourcing
www.sfiprogram.org
SFI-00993
Logo Applies to Text Stock Only

# Contents

# Introduction

> ## "In the kitchen . . . I have it together."
>
> Gabi Diamond,
> *Young & Hungry*

If you learn one thing from *Young & Hungry*'s Gabi Diamond, it should be that with a little skill and some simple ingredients, it's possible to cook your way out of anything. Okay, maybe not *anything*. Unfortunately, you can't pay off your student loans with nachos. But if you've broken girl code and accidentally made out with a guy your friend was eyeing at the bar, can you patch things up with an apology and a batch of brownies? Yes . . . yes, you can. Food is a cure. Food is a savior. The right food can get you through breakups, help you start a new relationship, or—if you're able to make your boss's favorite holiday pie—even get you a promotion. This book is going to show you how to get that promotion, decorate your apartment, meet a nice guy, make friends in a new city . . . and do it all while enjoying some yummy recipes that'll help you along the way. So get ready to learn some techniques for a full, amazing, delicious life.

# 1

# Life Basics for Not-So-Basic Babes

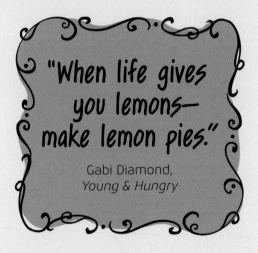

"When life gives you lemons— make lemon pies."

Gabi Diamond,
*Young & Hungry*

# Introduction

As much as everyone loves ordering pizza and crashing on their friends' couches, there comes a time in every girl's (or guy's) life when you realize that you need to learn how to cook and get yourself a decent apartment (key word here is *decent*). You don't need to cook like Julia Child, but you *do* need to learn some go-to recipes and have a well-stocked pantry. And your apartment doesn't have to be worthy of an *MTV Cribs* episode, with closets full of clothes and makeup; it just needs to have the necessities. Food and shelter: these are the basics. And the best thing about basics is that they can look (and taste) terrific without too much extra work. For example, this chapter has *five ways* to make a roast chicken. So for all you girls who have never stocked a pantry, gone grocery shopping, made coffee, decorated a home, or bought grown-up makeup or clothes, this is the chapter for you.

# Get Into Your Pantry: Stocking the Basics
## A Helpful Introductory List of Pantry Basics for the Modern Cook—Suitable for Even the Tiniest of Apartment Kitchens

The ability to cook is high up on the list of grown-up skills that everyone should have. A clean, well-stocked kitchen and essential culinary tools are the building blocks of producing tasty, healthy meals that don't drain your checking account.

And here's the thing: cooking can be easy and a whole lot of fun (more fun than going to a restaurant, in our humble opinion)! Even if you've never done it before. Even if you're kind of afraid of your stove. As with anything else, if you dive in unprepared, you are not likely to meet with much success. But with a few good tools, techniques, and ingredients, you can be cooking great food, saving money, and impressing the hell out of all your friends and potential *lovvahhs*.

The first thing you have to do is get your pantry or cupboards clean.

## Step 1: Clean.

Having a clean kitchen makes cooking significantly more enjoyable. Food keeps longer in a kitchen that is free of mold, bugs, and mice (gross, but more common than you'd think), and such parasites stay away from clean spaces. It's also much easier to clean up little messes when your kitchen itself isn't a big mess. A clean kitchen is easy to acquire and requires less effort than you might think. You'll need:

- 3 sponges (1 for dishes, 1 for counter, 1 for scrubbing)
- Multipurpose cleaner (diluted white vinegar scented with a little lemon or lavender oil in a spray bottle makes for a totally effective, cheap, and environmentally friendly option)

- A broom
- A mop
- Paper towels or a whole bunch of clean dish towels
- Dish soap (dilute a little castile soap for a greener option)

Take everything out of your pantry/cupboards. Consider each item and determine if it's still good and something you'll ever eat. If it's neither, toss it; if it's both, keep it. If it's still good but you'll never eat it (and it's unopened), donate it to your local food bank. If it's been opened but you'll never eat it, attempt to pawn it off on your friends/roommates, but if you're unsuccessful, toss it (composting if possible).

Before you put all the dry goods you're keeping back on their shelves, use the abrasive back of a wet sponge to scrub all the grit from the shelves. (Three-year-old spilled, dried, crusted-over honey will make your pantry like Club Med for fruit flies—not a good thing.)

Once all the yuck has been removed, spray the shelves with multipurpose cleaner, wipe it away, and put back the dry goods you're keeping.

## Step 2: Stock.

These are the shelf-stable items you will return to over and over again. When you have them on hand, you need only to pick up a few fresh ingredients (fruit, vegetables, meat or fish, tofu, eggs, etc.) to put together a tasty, healthful homemade meal.

Obviously, if you are vegan or gluten-free or your dietary restrictions prohibit any of these ingredients, you should adjust your pantry accordingly.

- Unbleached all-purpose flour (usually around $4.50 for a 5-pound bag)
- Extra-virgin olive oil (make sure to always buy olive oil labeled *extra-virgin* and get something you enjoy the taste of) $6.50 for 12 ounces

- Vegetable/canola oil (coconut oil is a good option here, too, but it's generally a bit pricier) $4 for 16 ounces
- Kosher salt ($3 for 24 ounces)
- Black pepper (look for the kind that comes in a grinder) $2
- Baking soda ($3 for a 6-ounce can)
- Baking powder ($3 for a 6-ounce can)
- White granulated sugar ($3 for a 16-ounce box/bag)
- Brown sugar ($2.50 for a 16-ounce box/bag)
- Honey ($4 for 8 ounces)
- Balsamic vinegar ($4 for 12 ounces)
- Natural peanut butter (creamy or crunchy, your choice) $4.50 for 12 ounces
- Mayonnaise (store it in the fridge after opening) $3.50 for 16 ounces
- Garlic ($0.50 for a head)

**NOTE:** the costs listed above are approximate and will vary from store to store.

# Save Your Dough:
## How to Save Money at the Grocery Store

**Shop mostly on the outside aisles.** The aisles around the perimeter of the store typically contain the bulk section, the produce section, the meat and seafood counters, and the dairy and egg refrigerator cases. These are generally the healthiest and least expensive items in the grocery store. The prepared, processed, and packaged foods tend to be the high-ticket items. Buy these sparingly.

**Ask the butchers and fishmongers to help you out.** In addition to being knowledgeable about the products they sell, the people behind the meat and seafood counters are the ones who clean, debone, skin, fillet, grind, and trim the proteins they sell. Don't be shy about asking them to do some of the prep work for you. If whole fish are on sale, buy them (they're much cheaper per pound than skinned, precut fish fillets or steaks), and have the fishmonger clean, skin, and fillet them for you, free of charge.

**Buy in-season produce for the best prices.** There's a simple reason why a locally grown tomato costs less in July than a flown-in-from-Chile tomato in January: airfare. Buying fruits and vegetables grown close to home (which is only possible when they're in season) costs less, because the produce doesn't have to travel as far.

**Learn to love the bulk section.** Some of the best deals at the grocery store can be found in the bins of the bulk section. When you buy in bulk, you are paying only for the food itself, not packaging, so the pricing is significantly lower than prepackaged goods. It's great for when you need a lot of something, but it's also wonderful for when you need only a little. (Why buy a 24-ounce package of cashews when you only need a quarter cup of them for a recipe?) It's worth the annoying 12 seconds it takes to wrap a twist

tie around a plastic bag and write the product code on it. Invest in a pack of cheap jumbo-sized mason jars to store things like flour, sugar, rice, beans, pasta, oats, nuts, and dried fruit from the bulk section. Keeping them in an airtight container like a mason jar will keep them fresh longer.

**Shop often and in small increments.** Of course, frequent shopping isn't possible for everyone, but a great way to grocery shop is to keep the pantry stocked with nonperishables and then augment a few times a week with small quantities of fresh items: a piece of meat or fish here, some cheese and eggs there, and whichever fruits and vegetables are ripe and in season. It means more frequent stops at the store, but when you can, this is one of the most cost-effective ways to shop. Since it requires you to grocery shop on an as-needed basis (as opposed to filling a cart with enough food for two weeks), you are far more likely to actually use all of what you buy. (How many times has the kale you optimistically bought a week ago been left to turn to mush in your crisper because you never got around to eating it?) Nothing is sadder than a compost bin full of never-used produce gone bad.

# Just Brew It:
# How to Make Coffee at Home
## (So You Don't Spend Your Rent Money on Lattes)

That morning latte you stop for every day on the way to work may not seem like an expensive indulgence, but $4 per day over the course of a year adds up to over $1,500! That's a lot of cash for morning coffee.

"But I don't have the money/room/patience for a coffeemaker!" you say. Undestood. But guess what? You can make great coffee at home even if you don't have one, with tools you probably already have on hand. You'll need a mug, a measuring spoon, and a fine mesh strainer. Oh, and ground coffee and water. Here's what to do:

1. Fill a heatproof container (like a mug or a mason jar) with 2 tablespoons ground coffee for every cup of boiling water.
2. Pour boiling water over the ground coffee.
3. Let the coffee and water steep for 5 minutes, stirring once or twice.
4. Using a fine mesh strainer, strain the coffee right into the mug(s). Add milk and/or sugar if desired, and drink right away.

# Roast Chicken Five Ways

## (Plain; Garlic, Lemon, and Rosemary; Hoisin; Barbecue; French Kiss)

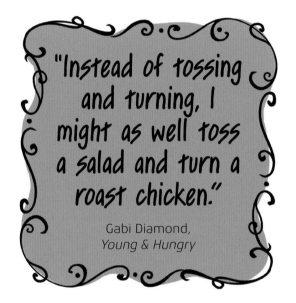

"Instead of tossing and turning, I might as well toss a salad and turn a roast chicken."

Gabi Diamond,
*Young & Hungry*

Now that you've learned how to make killer coffee for breakfast, it's time to learn how to throw together a great dinner. What's great about chicken is that, in general, it's universally liked (you're not likely to hear any "I'm allergic to chicken" nonsense), and it's relatively easy to make. Plus, roast chicken makes for some pretty sweet leftovers the next day. So here are some tasty roast chicken recipes that you can make for yourself, your friends, or the guy you just met on Tinder. You may not have a thigh gap, but you've got some chicken thighs, and that's so much better.

# Basic Roast Chicken

Prep Time: 5–10 minutes      Cook Time: 50–55 minutes      Serves: 4–6

## Ingredients

**1** 3½–4 pound roasting chicken

**1** tablespoon salt

**1** tablespoon ground black pepper

**2** tablespoons extra-virgin olive oil

## Directions

1. Preheat oven to 450°F.

2. Remove any innards from inside the chicken (usually in a small bag). Discard.

3. Pat the chicken all over with a paper towel.

4. Set the chicken in a roasting pan or cast iron pan, breast side up.

5. Season all over with the salt and pepper, including inside the cavity of the chicken.

6. Rub with olive oil.

7. Roast in the center of the oven for 50–55 minutes, or until very golden brown.

8. Let rest for 5 minutes, then cut apart and serve.

# Garlic, Lemon, and Rosemary Roast Chicken

Mix the olive oil with 2 cloves of finely chopped garlic, the chopped leaves of a sprig of fresh rosemary, and the juice and zest of one lemon. Rub all over the chicken after seasoning it with salt and pepper, then roast as directed.

# Hoisin Roast Chicken

Instead of salt and pepper, rub the chicken all over with 3 tablespoons hoisin sauce (usually found near the soy sauce in grocery stores, or in Asian specialty markets). Skip the olive oil, and roast as directed. Brush with more hoisin after roasting, if desired.

# Barbecue Roast Chicken

Instead of salt and pepper, rub the chicken all over with ¼ cup prepared barbecue sauce. Skip the olive oil, and roast as directed. Brush with more barbecue sauce after roasting, if desired.

# French Kiss Chicken

Prepare the chicken as directed with salt, pepper, and olive oil, then pat the whole thing with 3 tablespoons Herbes de Provence. Roast as directed.

# There's No Place Like Home:
## Making Your Place Pinterest-Worthy, Starting with Your Kitchen

You have an apartment! Yay, you. You are no longer living in your car, in your parents' basement, or on your best friend's couch. This is a real step up. First apartments are not going to be perfect. Just look at Gabi and Sofia's place on *Young & Hungry*. It's a one-bedroom (for two of them) and there's very little space. Yet their apartment is  so warm and inviting because they have the right colors, furniture, and layout. They used some decorating tips that you will also learn in this section.

Remember, it's your first apartment, not your dream home. Like Gabi and Sofia's, it might be a walk-up, but on the plus side, you won't need a gym membership. It also might not have air conditioning (**HINT**: Find a friend who does have it), but it's your apartment, so it's up to you to dress it up. And it's fun! You're finally living somewhere *you* get to call the shots. And it's important that you like where you live. So follow these helpful, timeless tips for decorating on a dime.

## The Kitchen

**Focus on the fridge:** It's important that you want to spend time in your kitchen. The easiest way to make your kitchen look cute is to decorate that fridge. Go to your phone, print out some pictures of you with your friends and family, and put them into magnetic frames. You can even use a cute Snapchat filter on your pictures to give them some flavor. Another great idea: buy some magnets from places you've visited. It's a great conversation starter when a new guy comes over. *"You've been to Arizona? Me too!"* There's also something nice about putting invitations to weddings and other special events on your fridge so you have reminders of things you're looking forward to.

**Chalk it out:** Chalkboards make a kitchen complete. They're great for keeping track of things. For example, you can write your to-do list or messages to your roommate, like *Stop eating my ice cream!* Or if you're going to a farmers' market, you can remind yourself what you need to buy. Even better: if you're having a dinner party, there's nothing more adorable than writing the menu on a chalkboard in the kitchen for your dinner guests to see.

## The Entryway/Living Room/Dining Room

**Give yourself a warm welcome:** Walking into a cozy home is the best feeling in the world. A welcome mat with a cute slogan immediately makes your place feel like it's your own. A scented candle or freshly cut flowers also help set the mood.

**Goodwill should be called Greatwill:** You can get some insane deals at Goodwill. Remember, as fun as it is to "make it rain" at IKEA, stick to secondhand stores and Craigslist for some steals. Here are some of the items you should be looking for:

- **A couch:** Preferably a pullout, since you will probably have some visitors.
- **A coffee table:** Doesn't need to be fancy, but something that draws attention is always nice.
- **A dining table:** As long as your table can comfortably fit four people, you're okay.
- **Chairs for dining table:** Depends on the size of your table, obviously, but four chairs should work just fine.

- **Some pretty lamps:** Something edgy with a unique pattern or color can definitely bring the room alive.
- **End tables:** These are small tables that fit nicely next to your couch.
- **Bookshelves:** How else are you going to display this book for your friends to be jealous of?

**If you can, paint:** Some apartments do not let you paint, so first call your landlord or check your lease and make sure it's cool. If it is, get started! There are a million tips for painting on YouTube, so definitely watch some videos first. Then make sure to buy painter's tape (to create borders for ceilings, baseboards, and doorframes) and don't forget to wear the proper clothes. Remember that white shirt you never wear because you spilled red wine all over it? Wear it for painting! Your clothes are going to get dirty, so paint in clothes that you don't care about ruining. And to make painting more fun, invite some friends over to help you!

Pay special attention to color, since it's one of the first choices you can make to give your apartment some character. Did you know that a lot of restaurants paint their walls red because red is supposed to make you hungry? What colors do you like? An off-white is plain but sophisticated. Cooler colors, like greens, blues, and grays, are Zen and can help you relax. Think about what mood you want your apartment to reflect.

**Try temporary wallpaper:** It's so easy to put on or take off, and the best part is it's cheap and noncommittal. From vintage '70s prints to fun pop art, the best thing about temporary wallpaper is that you're not married to it. If you buy some psychedelic pattern and then want to change things up after three months, you can.

**Show off your personality:** If you're really into music, go down to the local record store (or if it's out of business, try eBay) and get some record jackets to put on the walls. If you like sports, frame a jersey from your favorite team. It's important that your place has personality—not just for you to enjoy, but for when guests come over, too. You want your guests to feel they get a sense of *you* when they walk in.

**Stop and think before buying expensive furniture pieces:** Just like you can fall in and out of love with a guy you meet on Bumble, you can fall in love with a piece of furniture . . . and then regret buying it. We've all done this. You see a bright pink sheepskin rug. It's out of your price range, but you splurge anyway. Next thing you know, you're introducing your rug to your friends, seeing it every day, and suddenly . . . you don't like it as much. Whenever you're thinking about buying an expensive piece of furniture, give yourself two weeks to think about it.

**Ain't no shame in a good frame:** When you're in college, it's totally acceptable to hang a poster with some Scotch tape. But when you're really trying to make your apartment look nice, a solid frame can make even the cheapest poster suddenly look expensive.

## The Bedroom

**Buy a big-girl bed:** Do yourself a favor and get yourself a big-girl bed. Growing up, you probably had a twin bed or a bunk bed, but now that you are an independent person, you deserve to live life to the fullest . . . with a full-size bed.

**Splurge on bedding:** You sleep in your bed every day (unless, well, you get lucky and have an away game), and because your bed is so important, investing in some bedding that's comfortable and pleasing to your eye is a must.

**Throw down the pillows:** Throw pillows with positive slogans on them make for great bedroom pillows. Plus, throw pillows give your bed a more grown-up vibe.

## The Bathroom

**Bath mats are essential:** But definitely only buy them in dark colors, because those things get dirty fast!

**Shower curtains make the room:** A shower curtain in a bright color can definitely make your bathroom a cheerier place to be.

**Put your shower stuff in fancy bottles:** This one takes time, but if you really want to make your bathroom feel ultra-luxurious, put your shampoo, conditioner, and body wash in uniform bottles.

Now that your bathroom is perfectly decorated, let's discuss what you likely spend most of your time in the bathroom doing . . . putting on makeup.

# A Good Foundation

> "How am I gonna have time to put on all my makeup so I look natural . . . you know, like I just woke up?"
>
> Gabi Diamond, *Young & Hungry*

You don't need to look like a Kardashian to love makeup. Not that there's anything wrong with the Kardashians. (Those girls know how to *werk*.) But when you look good, you *feel* good. And the beauty of being a girl is that when you have a pimple, you can cover it up. When you're on the best date of your life and it goes till four in the morning and you have huge bags under your eyes, you can hide those, too.

Girls love it when guys tell them *"You're so pretty without makeup."* Yes, that's true. But wearing makeup isn't about looking good for guys—it's about feeling good about yourself. Who doesn't feel better with a little coat of mascara, a tiny bit of blush, and some lip gloss? Plus, makeup should be for enhancing your good features (your sexy eyes and pretty lips, for example) and hiding anything you don't want the world to see (your under-eye bags and zits). Here are some basic makeup tips as well as some homemade beauty recipes, in case you can't afford to go out and get a facial (and let's face it, that money would be better spent on food).

## What Should Be in Your Makeup Bag?

- **Foundation:** Always test it on your jawline, not on your hand. Your hand is usually a few shades darker than your face. And ladies, for the good of your skin, try not to wear foundation to the gym. It clogs your pores and looks terrible running down your sweaty face.

- **Concealer is a gift:** Buy your concealer one shade lighter than the rest of your face and layer it on until your raccoon eyes become bright eyes. It's also handy to keep concealer in your desk at work for those late nights at the office.

- **Bronzer:** The best thing about bronzer is that it can give you a nice sun-kissed look without your ever having to hit the beach (or be around those harmful rays).

- **Blush:** A good blush makes you look sexy, glowing, and awake.

- **Eye shadow:** Neutral shades like light gold are fantastic because they look good on every skin tone. Pro tip: dab some concealer on your eyelids first and then put on the eye shadow so it stays longer. Also, light-colored eye shadow (like white) on the inside corners of your eyes makes them appear bigger.

- **Eyeliner is clutch:** For that sexy night out, go black and then take a cotton swab and smudge it. For everyday wear, brown is perfect because it's simple and looks natural. Remember that Cleopatra wore eyeliner, and she was one of the most famous (and sexy) female conquerors of her day.

- **Mascara:** Mascara is the best thing that has ever happened to womankind. Okay, that might be a little bit of an exaggeration. But even just one coat of mascara can make your eyes pop. Also, for big sexy eyes, buy two different kinds of dark mascara and layer them on. Mascaras usually have a specialty, so if one is good for length, the other might be great for color.

**NOTE:** During summer, get some waterproof mascara. The brand doesn't need to be fancy, but every girl has experienced going to the beach or the pool with a new guy and, the next thing she knows, looking like a psycho with mascara dripping down her face. Try not to look like a crazy person and get yourself some damn good waterproof mascara.

- **Lipstick:** Only go a few shades darker or lighter than your natural color. And remember, if you're going bold with the lip color, try to soften everything else and enhance one feature at a time to avoid looking like a clown.

## What are Some Ways to Beautify on a Budget?

- **Your lotion can double as an eye makeup remover:** Yup, ladies, it's true. The same lotion that you use for your legs can also take off that mascara and eyeliner. This trick comes in handy when you're staying at a hotel and you realize that you forgot to bring eye makeup remover. Or, try coconut oil. The same stuff you buy for the kitchen can double as both lotion and eye makeup remover.
- **If you have to choose between a manicure and a pedicure, go with the pedicure:** You get more for your money, and who doesn't love

someone pampering their feet? Plus, your fingernails can look great with a quick trim and a buff at home.

- **If you just got your hair blown out (and you like it):** Invest in some dry shampoo. You can extend your blowout for another couple of days.
- **Skip the blowout:** If you're on a major budget and you can barely afford to get a haircut, ask for just the cut and blow out your hair yourself. You'll save some money.
- **For a free makeover:** Head to your local department store. You're going to have to buy something (it can be the ten-dollar eyeliner). In exchange, you'll get your makeup done and maybe pick up some tricks along the way.
- **Or even try Birchbox:** For ten bucks a month, you get beauty samples delivered to your door every single month. It's like your birthday comes twelve times a year.
- **If you're a girl who loves a spa day:** But you're a babe on a budget, try these two recipes and bring the spa to you.

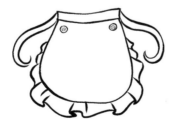

# Brown Sugar Body Scrub

Prep Time: 2 minutes

## Ingredients

**1** cup brown sugar

**¾** cup grape-seed oil

A few drops of vanilla extract or your favorite essential oil, if desired

## Directions

1. Combine all ingredients in a mixing bowl and stir until completely incorporated.
2. Transfer to an airtight container (like a mason jar with a fitted lid).
3. To use, scoop a generous palmful into your hands and rub all over your skin to gently exfoliate. Rinse well.
4. Remember to rinse out the bathtub or shower after use, as the oil can make the shower surface slippery.

**NOTE:** While this recipe only makes enough for a few uses, leftover scrub will keep in an airtight container for up to six months.

# Honey Yogurt Face Mask

Prep Time: 2 minutes

## Ingredients

**⅛** cup plain yogurt

**2** tablespoons honey

A few drops of your favorite essential oil (optional)

## Directions

1. Combine all ingredients in a mixing bowl until a creamy paste forms.
2. Remove any makeup from face and dry completely. Slather mask all over face (and neck if desired) and allow to dry (about 20 minutes).
3. Gently wipe off mask with a damp washcloth.
4. Rinse off completely, pat dry, and apply moisturizer.

**NOTE:** Leftover mask will keep in the refrigerator in an airtight container for up to a week.

# Keep Calm and Shop On:
## How to Shop, What to Buy, and Tips for Doing It on the Cheap

> "I'm trying to find the right outfit. I need something that makes me look professional, capable, and . . . like I didn't sleep with my boss."
>
> Gabi Diamond, *Young & Hungry*

You may have heard this before, but what you wear matters. It really does. Sure, your oversized sweatshirts and leggings are comfy, but don't even think about wearing them to the office or on a date. And what's worse than being too comfortable? Being *uncomfortable*. You know the feeling you get when you go to, say, a music festival, and you wear really short jean shorts because all the girls are doing it? You end up spending the whole time feeling self-conscious (all you're thinking about is whether or not people can see your cellulite, when in truth nobody else gives a crap) instead of enjoying yourself. The wrong outfit can literally ruin your experience. At the same time, the right clothes can put you in a powerful mindset. Who hasn't bought a new blazer and suddenly gone from feeling like a loser to channeling the next president of the United States?

This is where Catherine Cassidy comes in. Catherine's the CEO of Ustyled. Her company specializes in styling young professional women for work. But Catherine also cares about outfits that can transition from day to night. She took time out of her busy day to offer her top styling tips.

According to Catherine, **here's what every girl needs in her closet for work:**

- **A white blouse:** Now, your white blouse is going to look different from your mother's. But nevertheless, a nice white blouse can take you from your lunch hour to happy hour.
- **A nude heel and a black heel:** If you're really pinching pennies, these are the only two nice pairs of shoes you need.
- **A statement necklace:** It doesn't need to be expensive or gaudy. It just needs to be something that will stand out in the crowd.
- **Dark denim:** Doesn't matter the cut. You can go skinny, boot, or whatever best fits your body.
- **A cute cardigan:** This sweater also doesn't need to be expensive. It just needs to be the right layering piece.
- **A belt that fits:** Catherine thinks having a cute belt that you can tie at the waist is crucial to putting your outfit together.
- **A well-fitted suit:** If you have a more formal job, a full suit is necessary. But you can mix and match your suit pieces. If you work somewhere more casual, you can easily wear a well-fitted blazer with a good T-shirt and jeans, or a nice shirt with your suit pants.

**And for some nonwork items:**

- **Classic sneakers:** A cute pair of Converse sneakers can look fun at a baseball game or a casual brunch with friends.

- **Leather jacket:** You can wear a leather jacket out on a date, and a classic fit will never ever go out of style.
- **Little black dress:** The right LBD can take you from your cousin's bat mitzvah to your best friend's birthday party. Invest in one ASAP!
- **Two V-neck tees in different colors:** For mixing and matching with just about anything.
- **Cute flowy top:** A cute flowy top paired with tight jeans is the ideal first-date outfit. You won't look like you're trying too hard, and you'll feel like you can actually eat on the date, because you won't be wearing something too tight.

When shopping for clothes, here are a few rules that Catherine thinks every girl must adhere to:

- **Do not ever sacrifice fit:** According to Catherine, girls have a tendency to buy things on sale even if the fit isn't perfect. That's a big no-no. Catherine says the most important thing when buying clothes is how they fit your body.

- **Look for jackets with one or two buttons:** When buying blazers, always look for jackets with one or two buttons. Those types of blazers typically give more of a feminine shape than jackets without buttons that can give you more of a boxy look.
- **Know the difference between tight and tailored:** There's a huge difference between the two. When something is tight, it pulls and it doesn't make you feel good (remember those short shorts?). When something is tailored, it fits snugly without pulling. It simply grazes the body.

- **Make a clothes-shopping list:** When shopping, it's important to know what you need. Keep a list going on your phone of the items you still need to buy, like a jean jacket or a black sweater. That way, whenever you're shopping, you'll be more likely to stick to the things you need instead of buying something unnecessary.
- **It's the little things:** People notice details, and Catherine emphasizes how important it is to accessorize. Whether it's a scarf, a belt, or a necklace, accessories make the outfit and show that you put time and care into looking good.
- **Quality over quantity:** Often people care more about the amount of clothes they have rather than the quality. Catherine says that it's important to invest in yourself. What she means is, it's better to spend $50 on a top that you'll have for a long time than to spend $10 each on a bunch of things that won't make it past the first wash.
- **Dress for the job you want:** If you're an intern but you dream of moving up to executive assistant, don't be afraid to grab yourself a blazer and some statement jewelry to show the boss that you're a serious girl who's got what it takes to take on more responsibility.

So now that you've learned how to dress for success . . . let's talk about work. The next chapter is all about the place where you spend the most time: the office.

# 2

# Saucy and Bossy— The Best Career Advice You'll Ever Get

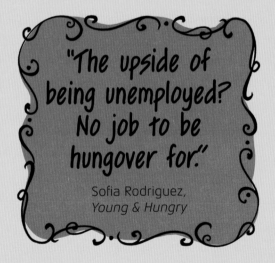

"The upside of being unemployed? No job to be hungover for."

Sofia Rodriguez,
*Young & Hungry*

# Introduction

Whether you're a barista, a banker, or a blogger, there are certain career tips that work for just about everyone. For example, do not break the copier. And if you do break the copier, lie and blame the intern. (Just kidding.) Or be smart when you're calling in sick. Don't make the same mistake as the girl who faked sick at work because her best friend was coming to town for a visit. She posted pictures of their adventures on Facebook, forgetting that she was Facebook friends with her boss. And also, should you even be friends with your boss on Facebook? It's so hard these days, because the lines are blurred like never before. Some people text their bosses. Should you do that, too?

Even though it's a lot easier to get ahead as a woman than it was when your mom was growing up, today's working girls have their own unique set of challenges. Like social media, for example. Like having your work e-mail on your personal phone, and feeling the constant need to check it, even on Saturday mornings when you're at brunch with your friends. Work has gotten so mobile that sometimes it feels like you're always at the office.

In *Young & Hungry*, almost every character deals with career challenges. Whether it's Elliot asking Josh for a raise, Sofia trying to find her passion, Yolanda feeling taken for granted, or Gabi sleeping with Josh (her boss) and then deciding whether or not she can still work with him, this chapter will address those issues and more. Maybe you've just graduated college and this is your first real job; maybe you're the summer intern, or maybe you've just started your own business. Whatever your position, get ready for some career advice that works.

# Skip Brunch and Pack a Lunch:
## Ways to Get By on a Small Salary

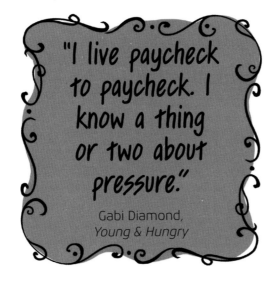

"I live paycheck to paycheck. I know a thing or two about pressure."

Gabi Diamond,
*Young & Hungry*

Unless you've created an app (hello, *Young & Hungry*'s Josh Kaminski) or won the lottery, you're probably not raking in the dough. It's pretty much a universal truth that first jobs don't pay much. Sadly, neither do most second jobs. It's really hard living on a small salary. A lot of women, in addition to their full-time jobs, babysit or drive for Uber to make extra cash. If you're a young working girl living in a city (or really anywhere) and trying to go out and look good, it's going to be expensive. You've got dates, new outfits, happy hour . . . and you still have to pay your bills and buy groceries. So here are some tips that'll help you save money and avoid going broke and getting your credit card declined—or, worse, cut up in your face. Keep your finances on track with a few simple rules and one delicious recipe.

- **Write down what you spend:** When going on a diet, you write down everything you eat and how many calories are in each food item. The same idea applies with money. You're going on a money diet, so write down everything you buy and how much it costs. **NOTE:** This is going to scare you. When you realize how much money you spend on little things, like coffee, haircuts, and that cute little purse you just had to buy . . . you might be overwhelmed. Give yourself a break here; you're learning.

- **Budget:** *Budgeting* is a really scary word. But at some point in your adult life you're going to have to go on a budget. If you're having a hard time creating your own budget, there are tons of websites that offer that service. Some of those sites will even sync to your bank and credit card so that every purchase is recorded, and they'll also tally up how much you have left in your grocery, clothing, and parking allowances.

- **Clothing swaps are your friend:** Few things in life feel as good as wearing something new. There's just a sense that comes with a fresh new outfit that makes you feel like a million bucks. However, since you don't have a million bucks, get that "new clothes" feeling for free with a clothing swap. Invite a few of your girlfriends over and tell each of them to bring three pieces of clothing they no longer wear. Everyone can trade, and by the end of the night, you'll have a brand-new outfit . . . for free.

- **Do not buy something online without Googling *student discount* or *coupon code*:** Occasionally websites have deals, and if you Google the website and the words *coupon code*, you just might find one.

- **Know your local happy hours:** Going out for dinner is expensive but also really fun. One of the first ways you can save money is to dine out only during happy hour.

- **Follow the 10 percent rule:** Every time you get a paycheck, try putting 10 percent of it into your savings account. Over time, that money will add up and you will be rich! Okay, you may not be rich. But one day, you may want to buy a house or a car, and you will be really glad you have that money saved instead of blown on scratchers.
- **Smart girls take leftovers:** Money isn't the only thing that should never ever be left on the table. Smart girls always take leftovers with them so that they can eat them the next day for lunch.
- **Pack your lunch:** If you buy a salad or sandwich for lunch every workday, it will probably cost you around ten dollars, which is fifty dollars a week! That is crazy. At least twice a week, pack a lunch. You're going to save some major cash doing that. Our favorite quick packable lunch is mason jar noodle soup. It's filling, easy, and a delicious way to enjoy a restaurant-quality lunch in the comfort of your cubicle.

# Mason Jar Noodle Soup

Prep Time: 10 minutes     Serves: 1

## Ingredients

**1** teaspoon chopped fresh ginger

**3** green onions, sliced thinly

**1** red bell pepper, sliced

**½** cup fresh spinach or kale, thinly sliced

**2** ounces dried vermicelli rice noodles

**½** chicken or vegetable bouillon cube

**½** lime

A few sprigs fresh cilantro and basil (optional)

Asian chili sauce, for serving (optional)

## Directions

1. In the morning or the night before, pack the ginger, onions, bell pepper, greens, vermicelli, and ½ bouillon cube in a 12-ounce heatproof jar (a mason jar with a fitted lid is ideal).

2. Pack the lime, cilantro, basil, and chili sauce separately (or better yet, keep them at work/school).

3. At lunchtime, add enough boiling water to come to the top of the packed jar.

4. Give the contents a good stir with a fork or chopsticks, then screw on the lid, being careful not to burn your hands.

5. Let sit for a minute, then uncover, squeeze the lime into the soup, and stir well.

6. Top with the herbs, add the chili sauce, and eat.

# Be the Oatmeal of the Office:
## Consistent, Delicious, No Drama

"I may have said a couple of things to my boss that were inappropriate for the workplace. Or any place."

Sofia Rodriguez, *Young & Hungry*

Everyone likes oatmeal. Why? Oatmeal is easy, fast, consistent, inoffensive, good for you, and a positive way to start your day. And do you want to know a little secret? Being liked is just as important as having talent. Maybe more so, actually. There are people who advance in their careers solely because other people like them. And then there are talented rock stars who never get ahead simply because people don't want to work with them. That's why this is the best career advice you're ever going to get: be the oatmeal of the office!

- **Be as likable as oatmeal:** Be friendly to everyone, from the receptionist to the boss. It doesn't matter what someone's job title is. And, for the love of god, know everyone's name. Yes, you've got a lot going on, but remember the security guard's first name, because not only is it polite and respectful, but it's good to have people on your side.

- **Get things done on time:** One of the things people like about oatmeal is that it's fast. Whenever your boss gives you a task, always ask for the deadline. That way you'll never hand in anything late.

- **Be appropriate:** Unlike cold pizza, oatmeal is a totally appropriate breakfast. So on that note, your outfits should be totally appropriate for work. Reread our last chapter for wardrobe tips, but remember the three Cs: no cleavage, crop tops, or cutoffs.

- **Find your blueberry:** Oatmeal always tastes better with a little blueberry. A mentor can be your blueberry. Find someone in your field who's a little more experienced and ask that person out for coffee. Ask the questions you've been struggling with at work, and you'll be surprised how happy people are to give advice.

- **Use your oatmeal-fueled brain:** You know that person in your office who zones out all day on Facebook or watches videos online instead of working? Don't let that be you. Oatmeal is brain food, so if you're eating your oatmeal, your brain should be at top performance. Ask questions, go the extra mile, and take notes. When your boss gives you a list of tasks and you don't write anything down, do you look like a genius with an unbelievable memory, or do you look like someone who doesn't care enough to take notes? (**HINT:** The latter.) So grab a notebook or iPad and make sure that every time you get a new task, you write it down.

- **Always have a consistently happy attitude:** This is a big one. In your first couple of jobs, you're probably not going to be given exciting or hugely important tasks. In fact, it's more likely to be duties like taking out the trash, walking your boss's dog, watering plants, getting the mail, paying bills, and ordering supplies. Are any of these things glamorous? Nope. But just as oatmeal is always warm, happy, and delicious . . . so are you. Take out the trash, do it with a smile, and make some damn oatmeal!

# Overnight Oatmeal

Prep Time: 5 minutes, plus 5–8 hours in refrigerator          Serves: 1

## Ingredients

**1** 6-ounce carton of plain yogurt (any fat percentage is fine)

**2/3** cup regular rolled oats

**2/3** cup milk (any fat percentage is fine, or use nondairy milk)

Fresh fruit (optional)

## Directions

1. In a large bowl, mix together the yogurt, the rolled oats, and the milk.

2. If desired, add berries, sliced bananas, or any other cut fruit you like.

3. Scrape into a pint-size mason jar with a fitted lid.

4. Cover the mason jar with its lid and refrigerate for at least 6 hours (and up to 3 days).

5. Eat, topping with more fruit and/or yogurt if desired.

# I Made Out with My Coworker . . . and Other Office Don'ts

"Do act professional. Don't have sex with your boss. Do wear pants. Don't take them off."

Sofia Rodriguez, *Young & Hungry*

There are certain things that you should know never to do at work: make out with your coworker, take personal calls, or ask the receptionist to check your weird mole. Sure, we've all done them. (Okay, maybe not the last one.) But there are certain office mistakes that people make time and time again. To help you, here's a little list of things *not* to do if you want to get ahead.

- **DO NOT . . . make out with your coworker:** On the first episode of *Young & Hungry*, Gabi does something that 56 percent of people say they have done: be romantic with a coworker. It happens a lot. After all, you spend most of your time at work; it makes sense that, after a while, you start looking differently at Freddie from accounting. Sure, he's got a weird eye, and if you saw him on Tinder you might swipe left. But after weeks of having him help you fill out expense reports, he begins to look pretty good. Pro tip: do not make out with him. Most of these things don't end well. And they usually end with someone having to leave their job. So unless you think you and Freddie from accounting are going to get married and have lots of babies, don't be tempted!

- **DO NOT . . . take personal calls at work:** There's always that one person who fails to adhere to this rule. You've shared an office with her. You've heard her talking about her weekend of getting "soooo wasted." And all you want her to do is shut her mouth. Don't be that girl. If you really need to take a personal call at work, leave the building.

- **DO NOT . . . get drunk at work events:** Okay, the words *open* and *bar* make a beautiful combination. Who doesn't love an open bar? Especially at the company Christmas party. But do not make the mistake of getting hammered at work events. It doesn't matter how good the cosmos are . . . it's not worth it. Have one drink and then sip on club soda.

- **DO NOT . . . steal people's food from the fridge:** Fridge stealers are the scum of the earth. You know that feeling when you order pad thai and you don't eat the whole thing and you think, *I'm going to save half of it and bring it to work tomorrow,* and then when you go to get your pad thai from the work fridge . . . it's gone? You make it your mission to find out who ate your pad thai and you hate that food stealer forever. Do not be the person who ate the pad thai. You will be hated forever.

- **DO NOT . . . steal office supplies:** Someday, you may get desperate enough to steal toilet paper from work. It happens (hopefully not more than once). But if you keep taking toilet paper and other items from the office supply closet, pretty soon you turn into a thief. And you know what happens to thieves? They get fired.

- **DO NOT . . . have a messy desk:** This one is really hard, because a lot of people are organized in business but messy in life. However, when your desk is messy, people may get the impression that you're disorganized, and that perception could make it more difficult to get promoted.

- **DO NOT . . . write about your job on social media (unless that is your job):** Some people have jobs where their actual career is writing about their office on social media. Unless that is your job, do not write about your office on social media. You're going to regret it. Resist the urge to post comments (especially bad comments) about your office on Facebook or send a Snapchat of your boss having a bad hair day. On a related note, what do you do if your boss friends you on Facebook? This is a hard one, because you don't want to seem like a bitch for not accepting your boss's friend request. Our advice is to accept the request, but give your boss limited access so he/she can't see every single thing you're doing.

- **DO NOT . . . reply all without checking who's on the e-mail chain:** Sending out sensitive information to the wrong person is something you'll never live down. Before you hit "reply all," take a look at who else is on the e-mail.

If you avoid all these crucial errors, you'll be setting yourself up for success.

# Don't Cry; Make Everyone Pie:
## Rules for Navigating Office Politics, Plus a Recipe for Hand Pies

Since when did your office turn into an episode of *Game of Thrones*? One day you're thinking how great it is that you're working at a place where everyone is nice and treating you so well, and the next day your boss has called a meeting and invited everyone into the office. Everyone except you. Yup. It's happening. You are the victim of office politics. And it happens to everyone. Just look at Gabi in *Young & Hungry*. Elliot isn't exactly her biggest fan. He's constantly insulting her and putting her down at work, and Gabi has to find a way to handle it. Instead of running to the bathroom to cry and call your mom—or worse, writing a Facebook post about how you hate everyone at work—follow these simple rules.

- **If someone hates you, take that person out to lunch:** It might sound counterintuitive, but sometimes when someone doesn't like you, it's for a stupid reason that can be cleared up in a matter of minutes. For example, maybe you sat in a coworker's usual seat and that really pissed her off, but you had no idea. Over lunch, you can get to the bottom of it. Easy! When you're in a tricky situation, take that person out to lunch and charm the pants off her (but not literally—see the previous section if you have any questions about that).

- **Talk it out:** Maybe one of your coworkers called you out on something and copied the boss. It's awful. Instead of firing back an e-mail and hitting "reply all," simply walk over to your coworker's desk and explain what happened. In-person conversations are almost always better than e-mails, and there's no paper trail.

- **Don't go out with your work friends:** It's true that a lot of great friendships start at work. But before you and Brenda from HR go out and hit the town together, there are a few things you should be aware of. Friendships are complicated. And even if you're friends with people at work, try not to go out and drink too much with them. As a friend, Brenda from HR may *love* hanging with you, but too many crazy weekend nights and she'll start confusing your personal life with your professional one.

- **When someone steals your idea:** This has happened to everyone. You have a great idea for something, you tell it to a coworker, and suddenly they're taking credit. First talk to your coworker about it. Explain that you're really upset by what happened and try to see if it was a misunderstanding. If it's something bigger than a misunderstanding, go to someone above you in rank to resolve the situation.

- **Do not gossip about coworkers:** There's always office gossip. In fact, most people are at least somewhat guilty of it. But you do not want to be known as the office gossip. Do not engage. When someone starts gossiping, look at your phone, find some random e-mail, pretend it's urgent, and walk away!

- **Make people a little something for their birthdays, baby showers, etc.:** People really appreciate it when you remember major milestones in their lives. But you don't need to buy your boss something expensive on his or her birthday (in fact, you shouldn't—when you buy something expensive, you end up looking like you're trying too hard). Instead, try this recipe for handheld pie. It works for birthdays, engagements, new babies, or basically any other occasion. Plus, who doesn't love a little pie?

# Hand Pies

Prep Time: 20 minutes     Cook Time: 30 minutes     Makes: 6

## Ingredients

All-purpose flour or parchment paper

**1** standard store-bought piecrust (the kind that comes in a tightly rolled cylinder, not the kind already pressed into an aluminum pie tin)

## Filling ideas:

Jam

S'mores: miniature marshmallows, chocolate chips, and broken-up graham crackers

PB&J: peanut butter and your favorite jam/preserves

Lemon curd

Chocolate-hazelnut spread

Pumpkin pie: pumpkin puree, brown sugar, pumpkin pie spice, and a pinch of salt

Hot-pepper jam and cream cheese

Brown sugar and cinnamon

## Directions

1. Preheat the oven to 350°F.

2. Line a baking sheet with parchment paper or dust with flour.

(continues)

lemon

rasp

Choc →

3. Roll the dough out into a large rectangle, about ⅛ inch thick.

4. Use a wineglass or jar to cut the dough into small circles, about 4 inches in diameter.

5. To fill each hand pie, spoon 2–3 tablespoons of filling into the center of one circle of dough, leaving a border.

6. Wet your finger or a pastry brush with water, and dab it on the border of the dough.

7. Place a second circle of dough over the top of the filling.

8. Use your fingers to pinch the pieces of dough together to form a tight seal.

9. Use the back of a fork to gently pleat the edges of the dough.

10. Use the fork to poke a few holes on the top of the dough (this lets a little air escape and keeps the filling from exploding during baking).

11. Repeat with remaining dough and filling.

12. Arrange the hand pies on the prepared baking sheet. (Make sure there is space between them.)

13. Bake for 28–30 minutes, until golden brown.

14. Let cool for at least 5 minutes and serve.

# You've Got the Credentials, Now You Need the Essentials

Okay, now that you're officially killing it at your job, and you're on your way to being the next Sheryl Sandberg, Beyoncé, or Bethenny Frankel, you need the essentials. Here is a little list of things you're going to need as you kick off your heels and start climbing that ladder of success.

## Necessary Items for Your Desk Drawer

- Mint gum
- Tampons
- Headphones (so you can discreetly watch YouTube videos during your lunch break)
- Small toothbrush and toothpaste (in case you have onions and garlic for lunch, or get lucky and sleep at a guy's place)
- A change of shirt and underwear (in case you get lucky and sleep at a guy's place)
- Deodorant and a small perfume roller
- Over-the-counter pain reliever
- A PowerBar
- A stain-remover stick
- A hand mirror
- A pair of heels that you can live without but should keep anyway (in case you get a last-minute online date)
- POTTYMINTS (an air freshener for the bathroom that works great if you have to go number two at work and don't want anyone to smell what you did in there)

# What to Pack for an After-Work Date

You know the most frustrating part of dating? Not the texting (although that is very frustrating). . . . Not the mind games or the outfit changes. . . . It's the after-work date. Guys have stopped asking girls out on Saturday nights for first dates. They say it comes across as desperate. As a result, most of your first dates are probably on Tuesdays, Wednesdays, or, worse, Mondays. The hardest part of the after-work date? Not knowing when you're getting out of work. If you have to run directly from the office to the bar . . . here's what you need to pack.

- **Your date outfit:** Do not wear your date outfit to work! First of all, it might be too sexy for the office. Worse, you might stink it up if you're wearing it all day. And what if you're wearing a white blouse and you eat sushi at lunch and spill soy sauce all over it? Bringing a change of clothes helps you avoid a scary situation.

- **Dry shampoo:** Don't you hate it when your hair looks like a Pantene commercial in the morning and by the evening you look like the "before" picture in a makeover article? Ladies, dry shampoo is going to change your life. Brush your hair, spray on a little dry shampoo, and suddenly you will have so much less oil and a ton more *va-va-voom*.

- **Makeup bag:** You don't want your makeup to be too severe on a first date, so just freshen up with a light touch. A little concealer around the eyes, some blush, another coat of mascara, and you're good.

- **Sexy underwear:** Not because you're going to get lucky—although, hey, that would be nice—but because nothing makes a girl feel sexier than sexy underwear. So wear it, and suddenly you're a Victoria's Secret model.

- **A quick dinner:** The looming question about the after-work date is whether you'll be eating dinner on the date or just having drinks. It seems like most first dates are drinks, and if that's the case it's *really* important that you eat before you have a drink. No one wants to be the girl slurring her words after one glass of wine. So pack a dinner before a drinks date and eat it at the office. This recipe for a quinoa bowl with tofu and avocado is great, since it's fast and the contents can easily be stored in your work fridge.

# Quinoa Bowl
# with Tofu and Avocado

Prep Time: 10 minutes     Cook Time: 15 minutes     Serves: 4

## Ingredients

**1** cup quinoa

**2** cups water

**4** tablespoons extra-virgin olive oil, divided

**14** ounces extra-firm tofu, cut into 2-inch pieces

Salt

**2** tablespoons rice vinegar

**2** tablespoons soy sauce

**2** teaspoons honey

**1** avocado, sliced

**3** scallions, sliced

**1** red or green chili, sliced, for serving

## Directions

1. Combine the quinoa and the water in a pot over high heat.

2. Cover and bring to a boil.

3. As soon as it begins to boil, reduce the heat to medium-low and simmer for 15 minutes.

4. Meanwhile, heat 2 tablespoons of oil in a large nonstick frying pan over medium-high heat.

5. Season the tofu with ½ teaspoon salt.

6. Cook the tofu for 5 minutes, until golden on one side.

7. Flip and cook for another 4–5 minutes, until golden on the other side.

8. Combine the vinegar, soy sauce, honey, and the remaining 2 tablespoons of oil in a small bowl. Whisk until completely incorporated.

(continues)

9. Toss the quinoa with the dressing and divide into 4 bowls.

10. Top each bowl with tofu, avocado, scallions, and chilies.

11. Serve immediately.

Now that you've got your dream job and you're killing it, it's time to focus on your health. Our next chapter will help you stay healthy, whether you're at home, out and about, or even at the office.

# 3

# Be a Foodie but Still Work Your Booty— How to Be Healthy but Still Indulge

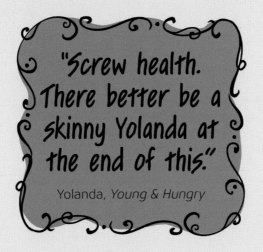

"Screw health. There better be a skinny Yolanda at the end of this."

Yolanda, *Young & Hungry*

# Introduction

You're a busy girl. Working, dating, Snapchatting. Who has time to do hot yoga every night for an hour? Not you. Remember that being healthy is not about being skinny (although it would sure be nice to be a size two and eat nothing but Swedish Fish and French fries). It's about being mindful of what you eat. (You can eat the Swedish Fish and French fries, but you can't have so much of them that you have to unbutton your pants.) Being healthy means treating your body nicely. Putting healthy, good food into it. Working it out. Calming it down. In *Young & Hungry*, everyone is constantly trying new ways to be healthy. Whether it's Gabi and Sofia doing a spin class together, Yolanda and Elliot trying a juice cleanse, or Josh going on a bike ride or kickboxing, those characters realize that when you feel good, you're a happier person. So that's what this chapter is about: being healthy and doing it quickly, easily, and inexpensively.

# When Harry Met Salad:
## How to Avoid the "I'm in a New Relationship" Ten Pounds

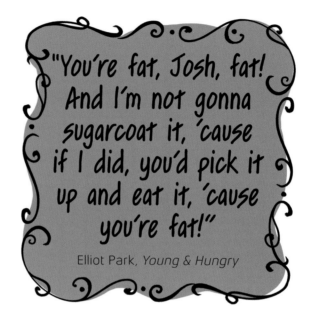

"You're fat, Josh, fat! And I'm not gonna sugarcoat it, 'cause if I did, you'd pick it up and eat it, 'cause you're fat!"

Elliot Park, *Young & Hungry*

There's something that happens to people when they get into relationships: they tend to gain weight. Call it happiness, call it love weight, call it whatever you want, but at the end of the day, you can't lie to your scale (although you probably have tried that already). Sure, weight gain in moderation isn't the worst thing in the world. But when you're dating a new guy and you're eating cold pizza at two in the morning, it might taste damn good, but it's not going to *feel* good when you wake up bloated and can't fit into your skinny jeans. So here are some ways that you can change your relationship status on Facebook without having to change the way you live.

- **Get seven to eight hours of sleep at night:** One of the hardest things to do in a new relationship is go to sleep. There's something really challenging about sharing a bed with a new guy (or girl). But it's important that you get enough sleep, so make sure when you're dating someone new that you call lights out . . . eventually.

- **Make working out a bonding activity:** One of the best things about being in a relationship is having someone to do things with. Make exercising one of those things. Instead of waking up on Saturday morning and heading to brunch with your boo, head to the park for a hike instead. Not only will it make you feel better, but it's also free.

- **Doggy-bag it:** Another fun part of dating someone new is that you will probably be going on some really fun dinner dates. And with fun dinner dates comes pressure to overeat. Instead of feeling the need to eat everything on your plate, have the waiter box up half of it.

- **Spend twenty minutes in heaven:** You probably played Seven Minutes in Heaven at a middle school party. You know, the game where a girl and a boy are picked to go into a closet and hang out there for seven minutes. Well, you and your man should play the same game after dinner, but for twenty minutes (since that's the amount of time it takes for your body to realize it's full). Instead of eating more after you finish a meal, fool around for twenty minutes. Only if you're still hungry then are you allowed to go back for seconds.

- **Try not to eat after 9 p.m.:** This is so hard, especially when you're dating. When it's Sunday night and you and your guy are cuddled up watching *Young & Hungry*, it's not easy to deprive yourself of a little microwaved popcorn. Well, instead of depriving yourself, switch to something a little lower calorie, like licorice or fruit.

- **Cook together:** Dating is expensive. Every time you guys go to dinner or out for ice cream, you're spending. That's a lot of money right there. One of the best ways to lose weight (without losing money) is cooking. It's something fun you can do with your partner. Try this recipe for watermelon salad pizza. It's not expensive, it's healthy, and it's a fun and easy recipe to make together.

# Watermelon Salad Pizza

Prep Time: 10 minutes        Serves: 4–6

## Ingredients

½ medium seedless watermelon (7–8 inches in
diameter)

⅙ medium red onion, thinly sliced

4 ounces feta, crumbled

1 handful fresh mint leaves

Juice of ½ lemon

4 tablespoons extra-virgin olive oil

Freshly ground black pepper

Salt

## Directions

1. Remove the ends from the watermelon and slice into four 1½-inch-thick rounds, then cut each watermelon round into 6 triangular slices, as if cutting a pizza.
2. Arrange the slices in a circle on 4 dinner plates, so it looks like you have 4 pink pizzas.
3. Top each "pizza" with the red onions, making sure to get some on each slice.
4. Scatter the feta over each pizza, making sure it is distributed evenly to each slice.
5. Do the same with the mint, scattering it over the slices, making sure there is at least one leaf on each slice.
6. Drizzle the "pizzas" with the lemon juice and olive oil.
7. Top with freshly ground black pepper and the tiniest sprinkle of salt (the feta is quite salty, so it only needs a touch of salt).
8. Serve immediately.

# Work Out in Your Office:
## Turn Your Desk into an Equinox

> "I jogged to the car dealership for free donuts, to the bank for free coffee, then to the coffee shop for free toilet paper."
>
> Sofia Rodriguez, *Young & Hungry*

You wake up late, stumble into the shower, get dressed, and get to work as fast as you can. That morning workout you had planned is so not happening. And you *want* to hit the gym later, but your friend invites you to happy hour. Well, a convenient time to exercise is after work . . . at your desk. You might want to wait until your colleagues have left, or you could corral your office mates into a little after-hours exercise. Celebrity trainer Jeff Paquet came up with some helpful moves that you can do at your desk after you've finished your workday.

1. **Triceps dip on chair:** Facing away from your desk chair, put your hands on the seat with your palms facing down and get into a squatted stance. With your elbows in, press down to lower your body for a full tricep dip. Make sure you try a couple in a squatted stance to feel the resistance, then gradually

walk your feet out to increase the resistance. Do 3 sets of 8–12 reps. Rest 30–45 seconds between sets.

2. **Standing push-up on chair:** Face the chair, and place your hands shoulder width apart on the seat for balance. Make sure your feet are together and far enough away from the chair so that your body forms a straight line. Then keep your elbows in and press up and down in a controlled motion. Do 3 sets of 8–12 reps. Rest 30–45 seconds between sets.

3. **Chair squats:** With your back facing the seat, stand far enough away from the chair to allow you to squat down to the edge of the chair and back to standing position. Do 3 sets of 8–12 reps. Rest 30–45 seconds between sets.

4. **Single-leg step-up on chair:** Place one foot on the chair and step up with the other foot. Switch legs. Do 3 sets of 8–12 reps. Rest 30–45 seconds between sets.

5. **Walk-up plank:** Start in a plank position with your hands shoulder width apart, your elbows and forearms holding you up. Starting with either side, press up to your hand on one side and then the other. Keep your stomach tight as you press up. Do 3 sets of 10–20 reps. Rest 30 seconds between sets.

6. **Up-down burpee:** Begin in a standing position. Drop into a squat position with your hands on the ground. Kick your feet back into a plank position while keeping your arms extended. Immediately return your feet to the squat position. Jump up from the squat position and repeat. Do 3 sets of 10–20 reps. Rest 30 seconds between sets.

7. **Single-leg hip-lift:** Lie down on the floor with your legs bent and lift one foot off the floor. Lift your hips up in the air, concentrating on contracting your butt muscles (think pushing through your heel). Make sure you keep the toes of your working leg up. Hold for a second or two and lower. Do 3 sets of 10–20 reps on each side. Rest 30–45 seconds between sets.

> "Wow, that's like two miles. You totally won't have to sneak into the gym later."
>
> Gabi Diamond, *Young & Hungry*

OTHER TIPS:

**Take the stairs:** Instead of riding the elevator at work every day, take the stairs. You'll be amazed at how many calories you burn.

**Try getting a standing desk:** Did you know that sitting is the new smoking? Okay, fine, sitting isn't as bad for you as smoking, but it's still not something that you should be doing for hours on end.

**Set an alarm on your phone for every two hours:** Then go take a walk. Walking is so important, even if it's just to and from the water cooler. . . . A little walking goes a long way.

**Invest in a Fitbit:** Fitbits can be expensive, so definitely check out eBay or a secondhand store to get one for cheaper. What's useful about Fitbits? You can't lie to them. It's so easy to say, "Oh, yeah, I totally walked ten thousand steps today," when in reality you probably walked ten. Fitbits force you to really examine how much exercise you're getting.

# How to Go from #Stressed to #Blessed

Stressful days are a fact of life. Maybe your boss is traveling to Italy for work and he's calling you at all hours of the night. Maybe someone stole your credit card and you're freaked out by the idea of never getting your money back (you will). It's really easy to work yourself into a state of crazy. The hard part is calming down from the stress. Here's a list of ways to lower your #stressed levels and up your #blessed levels.

- **Meditate:** It seems goofy, but meditation works. It helps you stay focused, helps you sleep, and helps you feel good. Meditation has all kinds of benefits. So download one of the guided meditation apps (most of them are free) and get your mind right.

- **Throw away your smartphone:** Okay, don't literally throw it away, but put it away somewhere where you won't see it for at least an hour before bed, because nothing gets your heart rate going as much as seeing all those stressful e-mails coming in.

- **Take a bath:** Baths are wonderful. They're warm, they're fun, and they keep you relaxed. So go get some lavender candles and prepare yourself for a nice luxurious bath.

- **Go for a walk:** Make yourself a relaxing playlist and take a stroll.

- **Say what you're grateful for:** If it works for Oprah, it'll work for you. Oprah is one of the biggest advocates of writing down what you're grateful for. As she says, "The single greatest thing you can do to change your life today would be to start being grateful for what you have right now." There have been several studies that show that acknowledging what you're grateful for improves your physical health and psychological well-being. So buy yourself a gratitude journal ASAP.

- **Sign up for a yoga class:** Not only is it a great workout, but many yoga poses are designed to keep you relaxed.
- **Drink tea:** There's nothing like a glass of chamomile tea to calm your nerves. Make yourself a nice hot cup of tea and allow yourself a minute to sip slowly and gather your thoughts.
- **Get a massage:** Yes, massages can be expensive, so if you don't have money (or time) for a full-body massage, go to a nail salon and ask if you can skip the polish and go right to the massage by the waiting area.
- **Call someone you love:** Sometimes just having someone to talk to is a great way to clear your head and relax. Whether it's your mom, your boyfriend, or your best friend, if you're feeling overwhelmed, give someone you love a phone call.
- **Watch something funny:** It's been proved that laughing can lower stress levels. So after a hard day at work, turn on your favorite episode of *Young & Hungry* and giggle until you feel better.

If you follow all (or at least some of) these tips, you will feel less stressed in no time.

# Pack a Snack and
# Look at the Mole on Your Back:
## A Practical Checklist

"You only have to worry if the doctor tries to hide bad news by using big words and medical terms."

Josh Kaminski, *Young & Hungry*

It's often not clear what doctors you need to see, or what to put in your medicine cabinet. Here's a practical checklist that you can use to stay healthy and make sure your body is running as smoothly as Josh Kaminski's Porsche:

## Doctor's Appointments:

- **The dentist:** Do yourself a favor and go every six months for cleanings, and make sure not to get unnecessary X-rays, since exposure to too much radiation isn't good for you.
- **The dermatologist:** Check yourself out naked and look for any new moles or sunspots. If you find any unfamiliar moles, take a picture of them next to a dime. That way you'll always have a reference point if

the mole gets bigger. Make sure to go once a year, and if you see any suspicious moles or skin discolorations, definitely call your doctor and make an appointment sooner.

- **The OB-GYN:** See your gynecologist once a year for a pap smear and pelvic exam. And if you're having sex with multiple partners, it's important to get tested for STDs every three months.

- **A general checkup:** According to Heidi Doyle, a physician assistant with Duke Primary Care North Hills, "If you're under thirty and healthy—don't smoke, no disease risk factors (including being overweight) and don't take prescription medications—get a checkup every two to three years." You should have your doctor check your:

  - Height and weight
  - Blood pressure
  - Blood work (for hormonal levels, blood sugar, blood count, cholesterol, triglycerides, and whatever else your doctor suggests)

- **Eye exams:** The American Optometric Association says you should get tested for eye issues once every two years.

## Things to Have on File:

- A list of drugs you take
- Any previous test results (blood work, STD tests, lists of vaccines you've had, or anything else that came up abnormal)
- An emergency contact
- Family's medical history (ask your parents about that)
- A list of questions you have for your doctor

## What You Need in Your Medicine Cabinet:

- Ibuprofen (Cures a hangover. Cures period cramps. Cures your life.)
- Eye drops (especially if you have contacts)
- Mini scissors (for cutting off tags)
- Rubbing alcohol
- Cotton balls
- Hair bands
- Q-tips
- Sunscreen
- An extra toothbrush (for when you get lucky)
- Floss

- Condoms (for when you get lucky)
- Throat lozenges
- A decongestant
- Cough medicine
- A thermometer
- A multivitamin
- Vitamin C
- Hydrocortisone cream
- Calamine lotion
- Bandages
- Tampons/pads
- Pepto-Bismol

## Things to Do Every Day:

- Brush and floss your teeth
- Eat something green
- Drink enough water (preferably eight glasses per day)
- Wash your hands (after the bathroom and before meals)
- Take a multivitamin
- Walk for twenty minutes
- Stretch (in the morning and at night)
- Sleep seven to eight hours
- Apply sunscreen
- Call one family member (It's not necessarily a health thing, but it'll make you feel good.)
- Pack a snack. It's always good to have a snack on the go. Whether you'll be at the office or on a road trip, bring something to eat with you. Try this recipe for coconut protein bites.

# Coconut Protein Bites

Prep Time: 1 hour and 10 minutes (includes refrigeration)     Makes: 20 bites

## Ingredients

**2** cups rolled oats

**10** pitted, dried Medjool dates

¼ cup water

¼ cup almond or peanut butter

**3** tablespoons unsweetened shredded coconut

**1** teaspoon vanilla

¼ teaspoon salt

## Directions

1. Put the oats in a food processor and pulse until they resemble coarse flour.

2. Add the dates, water, nut butter, coconut, vanilla, and salt and process until a sticky dough forms.

3. Line a baking sheet with parchment paper.

4. Scoop out mixture with a tablespoon, roll into balls, and arrange on the prepared baking sheet.

5. Chill in the refrigerator until firm (about an hour).

6. Serve.

# High School Reunions, Exes' Weddings, and Other Occasions When You Need to Look and Feel Great—Fast

High school reunions are stressful. You want to show up, look amazing, and tell the guy you had a crush on how fabulous your life has been since high school. Well, what if you're not quite at your fighting weight and you've got a reunion, wedding, or any other occasion creeping up a little too quickly? Here's what to do . . . and how to do it fast.

## Tricks to Conceal Weight Gain:

- **V-neck anything:** Whether it's a top or a dress, anything with a V-neck is going to pull attention away from your tummy and up to your cleavage. Big earrings and statement necklaces also help.
- **Heels:** Heels will help you with the stubby factor. But be careful not to buy shoes with ankle straps, since they cut you off. Another great tip is to buy shoes that are the same color as your skin tone so it will give the illusion of longer legs.
- **A spray tan:** Do not look orange, but nothing says healthy, glowy, and skinny like a really good (fake) tan.
- **Spanx:** A classic pair of Spanx is sometimes all you need to do the trick.
- **Don't go too baggy:** The worst thing you can do for your figure is wear something too big. You're going to look bulkier. Instead, opt for an outfit that's tailored but not tight.
- **Wear one color head to toe:** Doesn't matter what color, but wearing one color will make you look longer and leaner.
- **Define your waist:** A fitted dress can look even sleeker with a belt that cinches at the waist.
- **Put your hair up:** Having your hair up can help make a puffy face look thinner.

- **For a more casual event:** The most flattering outfit you can wear for a more casual event is dark jeans that cut just in the middle (low-rise will give you a muffin top and high-rise will make you look puffy) paired with a flowy top and a fitted, structured blazer.

## Slim Down Fast

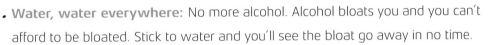

If you employ these tips one to two weeks before an event, you're sure to show up looking and feeling your best.

- **Water, water everywhere:** No more alcohol. Alcohol bloats you and you can't afford to be bloated. Stick to water and you'll see the bloat go away in no time.
- **Say no to sodium:** Sodium will also bloat you, so if you want things to get spicy at the reunion, say no to that spicy tuna roll.
- **Fiber up:** Fiber will help you go to the bathroom, which will help your body get rid of toxins that may be stopping your weight loss.
- **Protein and veggies are your friends:** Cut out the sugar. Instead of ice cream after dinner, how about a turkey slice?
- **Up your cardio:** Try running three to four times a week for thirty minutes, and girl, you are going to see some results.
- **Drink green tea:** Green tea has been known to boost your metabolism. *The American Journal of Clinical Nutrition* found that green-tea extract increases the metabolism by 4 percent over a twenty-four-hour period.

And remember one thing: you are not defined by what you weigh! It's not about the number on the scale, it's about feeling good about yourself. When you walk into an event, try to remind yourself of your unique nonphysical traits. For example, *I'm hilarious* or *I'm a kick-ass friend*. Now get your outfit ready and be prepared to make an entrance. One way to feel good about yourself is to give your body the gift of this green smoothie.

# Superfood Green Smoothie

Prep Time: 5 minutes          Serves: 1

## Ingredients

**1** banana

**2** cups de-stemmed, sliced kale

½ cup of coconut water (or regular water)

**1** cup blueberries or mango (fresh or frozen)

**1** tablespoon almond butter (or other nut butter)

## Directions

1. Combine the banana, kale, and coconut water (or regular water) in a blender.

2. Puree until smooth, about 1 minute. Add the blueberries or mango and the nut butter and puree for another 20–30 seconds, until smooth.

3. Pour into a glass and serve.

# Meet You at the Barre Class:
## Tips for Making Friends Part of Your Healthy Routine

Friends are big influences on what you do. You know how when one of your friends is on a food binge, and the next thing you know the two of you are on your way to get frozen yogurt after you just finished an entire pizza? Similarly, there's nothing more uncomfortable than going to dinner with one of your friends when she's on a new diet. You're at a sushi place, and she's getting two pieces of sashimi while you're chowing down on roll after roll. It's really important to make friends part of your healthy routine. Here are some ways to make working out with your friends more fun.

**Walk and wine night:** Walking and wine nights are great because they bring together three wonderful activities: catching up with friends, drinking, and walking. Unfortunately, only one of the three burns calories (**HINT:** It's not talking). Once a week, try a walk and wine night with your friends. Someone brings over a bottle of wine, and as a reward for all your exercise, you get to drink after the walk is over.

**Zumba:** Zumba is great because it's like a little party. You're dancing, you're sweating, and occasionally you get a hot single instructor. Zumba is an energetic and fun way to sweat with your girlfriends.

**Hit the club:** Dancing burns calories. An hour of dancing can burn around 443 calories. Instead of spending your Friday night going to the movies and splurging on the extra-large popcorn (with butter, of course), go to the club and get your freak on. You'll burn calories, hang with your friends, and who knows? Maybe you'll meet someone interesting.

**Do *The Biggest Loser* with your friends:** Who doesn't love *The Biggest Loser*? If you and your girls all want to lose a few pounds, do your version of

*The Biggest Loser* and make it a little competition to see who can lose the most weight. Loser has to buy everyone a healthy dinner.

**Try some social sports:** Sports like basketball, soccer, volleyball, and tennis are great because they're all very social. Try to organize a league or even just a monthly pickup basketball game with friends.

**Trade lemon ice for ice cream:** Instead of going out for ice cream or frozen yogurt with your girls, try this recipe for light & luscious lemon ice. You'll have a nice tasty treat without all the fat!

# Luscious Lemon Ice

Prep Time: 3 hours, 25 minutes (includes freezing time)     Serves: 4

## Ingredients

**1** cup water

½ cup granulated sugar

¼ teaspoon salt

Zest of 1 lemon

½ cup fresh or bottled lemon juice

Handful fresh mint

½ cup fresh blueberries, for garnish (optional)

## Directions

1. Combine water and sugar in a medium pot over medium-low heat. Bring to a simmer.

2. Simmer until the sugar is completely dissolved, stirring periodically. (This should take about 4 minutes.) Remove from heat.

3. Add salt and lemon zest, and let it steep for about 15–20 minutes.

4. Stir in the lemon juice.

5. Pour liquid in a shallow metal pan (like a loaf pan or an 8-inch cake pan).

6. Place in freezer and stir to break up the ice every 30 minutes for 3 hours. The consistency should be like slushy snow.

7. Serve immediately in dessert bowls, garnished with fresh mint and blueberries.

# 4

# Count Your Friends,
# Not Your Calories

"Friends don't tell friends they look like truck-stop prostitutes. Friends say, 'Hey, you look cute in that dress.'"

Gabi Diamond, *Young & Hungry*

# Introduction

Where would you be without your friends? Friends are the ones who make you laugh, take you out dancing after a breakup, buy you drinks when you get promoted, are honest with you about what you're wearing, and have your back no matter what. It's important that every girl has a friend she can rely on. Just look at Gabi and Sofia in *Young & Hungry*. Those girls epitomize true-blue friendship. Whether Gabi is making Sofia an online dating profile because she fears Sofia's not getting out there enough, the girls are teaming up to create a food truck called The Dumped Truck and going on *The Rachael Ray Show*, or Sofia is there for Gabi during the many times her relationship with Josh is "off again," those girls know what it means to be a great friend.

Boyfriends come and go, but friends are the ones who are there when you're crying in your car and you need someone to wipe away your tears and drive you to Pinkberry on a Saturday night. Maybe you're lucky and you've got a group of best friends that you've had since childhood; maybe you were in a sorority in college and you've got a strong network; or maybe you've moved to a new city and for the first time since college, you're totally scared and overwhelmed at the possibility of making new friends. That's what this chapter is all about. Keeping, making, and cultivating the thing that makes life worth living . . . friendship.

# You Moved Away, Now You Need a New Bae:
## How to Make New Friends and New Dishes

Congrats! You picked up your life and moved to a new city. You're scared, you're alone, and for the first time, you don't have friends or family to call on a Sunday when you're bored and need someone to go shopping with. But don't fret. Making new friends isn't that hard. Here are some suggestions for making friends when you're new in town and you don't quite have your crew yet.

- **Facebook is your friend:** When you move to a new city, go on Facebook and search for the town you're now living in. Facebook will give you a list of every one of your "friends" who's living in that town. Shoot them a Facebook message. *Hey (insert name here), I noticed you're now living in (insert city or town here). I just moved here. I know it's been a long time, but I would love to take you out for a drink and hear about your experience living here.* Everyone loves being taken out for drinks, and you'll be able to decide if your Facebook friend will become a real friend.

- **Get on the apps:** People are meeting friends with BumbleBFF. What is it? It's basically a way to use a dating app to find friends. You include pictures and a profile and start swiping for some new BFFs.

- **Join an organization:** Maybe you're into working out, or reading, or salsa dancing. Whatever it is, find what you like to do and join the club. You're guaranteed to meet like-minded people who have similar interests. There's a site called Meetup.com that's really great for this.

- **Throw a small party:** Once you know a few people, ask each of your new friends to invite one of *their* friends to a small party you're throwing. The best way to meet people is through other people, and throwing a party will help expand your circle.

- **Look in your building:** There could be some interesting people living there, especially if you live somewhere cool and young. Don't be afraid to strike up a conversation if you're both waiting for the elevator or getting your mail.
- **Ask for friend recommendations:** When people are single they have no problem asking their coworkers to keep them in mind in case they know anyone available. Do the same thing with friends. Tell your coworkers that you're looking to expand your circle and see if they'd be open to setting you up on some friend dates.

## What's an Ideal Friend Date?

If you've managed to meet a new friend, it's time to take your friendship to the next level: a friend date. Now, if you asked her to coffee or dinner, it would be nice if you picked up the check . . . so keep in mind it doesn't need to be someplace expensive. It just needs to be somewhere fun where you guys can get to know each other.

- **Pick somewhere quiet:** Maybe it's your local coffeehouse. Whatever it is, take your new friend somewhere you can actually hear each other talk.
- **Do your research:** Try to find out what your new friend is into. Maybe her Facebook is covered with pictures from the outdoor concerts she loves going to. Maybe she's on a charity board. Whatever it is, do some research to make sure you and your friend have common interests.
- **Everyone likes brunch:** If dinner seems like too much for a casual friend date, do something more laid-back, like brunch. Two mimosas later, and you and your new BFF will be bonding over the fact that you're both obsessed with *Young & Hungry*. Your new friend not a big drinker? Invite her over and try our recipe for strawberry basil lemonade.

# Strawberry Basil Lemonade

Prep Time: 5 minutes     Serves: 4

## Ingredients

**1** cup fresh lemon juice (about 10 lemons, juiced)

**¾** cup sugar

**4** cups water

**10** ripe strawberries, sliced

**⅓** cup fresh basil, sliced into ribbons

**½** cup vodka (optional)

## Directions

1. Combine the lemon juice, sugar, water, strawberries, and basil in a blender.

2. Puree until smooth.

3. Stir in vodka, if desired.

4. Pour over ice and serve.

# Girl Code and Rocky Road:
## Desserts and Basic Girl-Code Rules

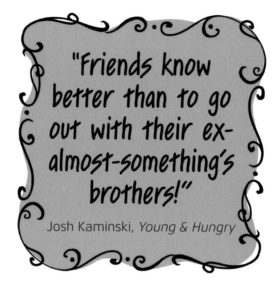

"Friends know better than to go out with their ex-almost-something's brothers!"

Josh Kaminski, *Young & Hungry*

Girl code is real, and if you break it, you're going to lose some friends. But the tricky thing is knowing what constitutes girl code. Here are the basic tenets of girl code.

**You shall not date a friend's ex-boyfriend:** This is a no-no. But then again, you shouldn't be stopped from connecting with your soul mate. So, if you're going to hook up with your friend's ex, you need permission. You need to call your friend and make sure that she's moved on and totally comfortable with you dating her ex. When Sofia hooked up with Jake, Gabi's ex, she didn't tell Gabi at first. When Gabi found out the truth, she was more disappointed than upset that Sofia didn't come to her first and ask for permission. The girls ended up making up, but the whole situation could have been avoided if Sofia had just talked to Gabi before hooking up with Jake. Learn from this!

**You shall drop everything to comfort a friend during a breakup:** Breakups are incredibly hard. Especially if your friend is the one who got dumped. No matter what you have going on in your life, if your friend just got broken up with, cancel your Saturday night plans and take your friend out on a date. Remember when Ruben dumped Sofia and Gabi spent the night eating ice cream with her? That's the kind of friend you need to be.

**You shall not leave the bar without telling friends:** If you and your girlfriends all go out together, you should all leave together. This is super important. Girls have to look out for girls. If you happen to meet the love of your life and you want to jet off to Paris, it's essential you ensure that the friends you came with have a plan to get home safely. If they're drinking, make sure they plan on calling an Uber. Just be certain they feel comfortable with your leaving.

**You shall like all pictures on social media:** This is a given, but if your friend just posted something on Instagram, support her and like the picture.

**You shall tell your friend when you hate her boyfriend:** This happens to everyone. Your friend started dating a new guy and she's obsessed with him. The only problem? You're not. The question is, do you tell her? Yes, because if you don't, no one else will. You have to realize, however, that there is a chance you could lose your friend as a result. Nothing creates a friendship war faster than when one friend doesn't like the other friend's boyfriend. And you have to hate him for a legitimate reason. Hating a guy because he's got bad style, or a bad hairline, or dorky friends, does not warrant an emergency sit-down session. However, if he's a bad person, a cheater, or unethical in any legitimate way you can think of . . . then yes, tell your friend that she needs to rethink her new guy.

**You shall not let your friend wear something unflattering:** This rule is major, and everyone's been there. Your friend just bought Kylie Jenner's lip kit and all of a sudden she's rocking the whole black matte lip thing, and it just does not look good. Who's going to tell her? You.

**You shall always bring brownies to girls' night:** This is crucial. You cannot show up to girls' night empty-handed. So instead, make this recipe for rocky road brownies.

# Rocky Road Brownies

Prep Time: 10 minutes     Cook Time: 28–29 minutes     Makes: 16 brownies

## Ingredients

Cooking spray or vegetable oil, for greasing the pan

**1** cup semisweet chocolate chips

**1¼** cups miniature marshmallows

**½** cup almonds, chopped

**½** cup (1 stick) unsalted butter

**1** cup sugar

**2** eggs

**1** teaspoon vanilla extract

**½** cup all-purpose flour

**⅓** cup unsweetened cocoa powder

**½** teaspoon baking powder

**½** teaspoon salt

## Directions

1. Preheat oven to 350°F.

2. Lightly grease a 9-inch-square baking pan.

3. In a mixing bowl, stir together the chocolate chips, marshmallows, and almonds. Set aside.

4. Put the butter in a large microwave-safe bowl. Microwave on high for 1 minute, until melted. (Alternately, you may melt the butter in a small pot over medium heat for 2–3 minutes, until melted, and then transfer to a large mixing bowl.)

5. Add the sugar, eggs, and vanilla and whisk until completely incorporated.

6. Stir in the flour, cocoa powder, baking powder, and salt until completely incorporated.

7. Pour the batter into the greased baking pan.

(continues)

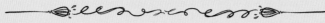

8. Bake for 20 minutes, then sprinkle the chocolate chip mixture over the top of the brownies.

9. Return the brownies to the oven for an additional 8–9 minutes, until marshmallows have softened and puffed slightly.

10. Let the brownies cool in the pan for at least 10 minutes before cutting.

11. Cut the brownies into 16 squares and serve warm or at room temperature.

# Roommate Hate (and Love):
## The Truth About Living with Friends

Living with people is really hard. It doesn't matter if you met your roommate on Craigslist or if she's been your best friend since elementary school; it's not easy when you choose someone and decide that the two of you are going to share a home. Maybe she's an early riser who wakes you up every morning as she's going to work. Maybe she hogs the TV when you're trying to watch *Young & Hungry*. Or worse, maybe she eats your food. Whatever it is, people have their quirks, and they may not bother you until you start living with them.

In *Young & Hungry,* Gabi and Sofia definitely have their fair share of roommate conflicts. Like when Gabi rented out their apartment so they could make some extra cash . . . without telling Sofia. Almost everyone's gone through the experience of meeting a newish friend and thinking that she would be the perfect person to live with, only to find out she has a freaky love of stuffed animals and invites random guys she meets on Tinder over once a week. The trick to living with someone is to have a clear set of rules and a clear way of dealing with conflict. So do yourself a favor and listen to these useful tips for living with someone new.

## List of Roommate Rules That You and Your Roommate Should Follow

**If you share a bathroom, do not abuse your shower privileges:** You shower, you dry your hair, and you're out. Taking forever in the shower is a sure way to piss off your new roommate.

**Boyfriend beware:** If you have a boyfriend who sleeps over a lot, be careful about how many times a week he's there. And you definitely need to have a conversation with your roommate to make sure she feels comfortable with someone else constantly hanging out in the apartment.

**Do your own damn dishes:** Don't expect your roommate to do them for you. Soon she will complain, and the next thing you know, you'll get home from work and she'll be meeting with people she found on Craigslist to take over your room.

**Knock-knock-knocking on your roommate's door:** If your roommate has the door closed, it likely means she doesn't want to talk to you or she has a guy over. Either way, respect the fact that her door is closed and she's doing something private, like talking to her mom (probably about you). If you desperately need her, be sure to knock on her door before entering her room.

**Yes, you're drunk, but don't eat her food:** So you go out and you come home drunk but there's nothing to eat. Nothing but your roommate's Ben & Jerry's Chunky Monkey. If you do make the terrible mistake of eating your roommate's food, don't forget to replace it. Not only is this rude, but it's also cheap. Buy her some freaking ice cream!

NOTE: The same thing applies for toiletries. You probably know people who never buy new shampoo or toothpaste because they're always using their roommates' stuff. Don't do this! And for the love of god, do not use your roommate's razor. Not only is it unhealthy, but it's just gross.

**You can't have friends stay for weeks at a time all the time:** You can't always have friends from home stay with you for an extended period. If you keep this up, your place is going to turn into a youth hostel for people who want a free trip. But if you are going to have friends staying over, make sure you give your roommate advance notice.

**Parties must be preapproved:** Always ask your roommate before you plan a party. What if she has a big work meeting coming up and you plan a party before telling her? Parties are definitely something that you need to discuss two to three weeks in advance.

**Don't borrow clothes without asking:** Although it seems like common sense, many people make this mistake. You took your roommate's jean jacket? It's going to get ugly when she starts looking for it. Gabi lost winning lotto tickets because she took Sofia's jacket and left it at her date's house. Always make sure to ask your roommate before you just take something of hers.

**If you're moving out, give notice:** If it's really not working out between you and your roommate, give her enough time to try to find someone new. A month's notice would be really kind. Also, if your roommate was the one who brought the TV, she's taking it with her when she leaves. As a rule, try not to split the cost of big-ticket items, like couches or televisions. It gets messy when one of you moves on, and suddenly the sofa you paid for half of is in the moving van. You can split up who buys what, but make sure you pay for 100 percent of every item you want to keep!

# One Who's Nice, One Who's Got Spice, and One with Advice:

## The Types of People You Need in Your Crew

"We're best friends, but we are nothing alike."

Gabi Diamond on Sofia Rodriguez, *Young & Hungry*

You don't need a ton of friends to be happy. You really don't. But you do need a core crew of friends who fulfill all your needs. This is a list of the types of friends who will really and truly round out your core crew.

**The crazy friend:** This is the girl who's always down for a good time. She's a partier and she knows where the action is. This is the girl you call after a breakup when you need to go out and let loose. She's probably not the same person you'd call for career advice, but she's the go-to gal when you really need to have a good time.

**The sweet one:** She'll listen to you cry for hours on end because she loves you, and is there for you, no matter what. She'll probably be the only one who will come when your car is stalled and you're stranded on the side of the road. Guard this friendship with your life!

**The older friend:** She's got words of wisdom and advice. Everyone needs an older friend (or mentor) who can tell you what to do in particular situations. She's been a bridesmaid at a wedding where she didn't like the guy her friend was marrying, and she got through it. She's made mistakes in her career and learned from them. Older friends are great friends because they have experience that you don't have.

**The guy friend:** Every girl needs a guy friend. Having a guy friend you can call to get a male opinion is so important. Guys usually know what other guys are thinking, and there's nothing like calling your guy friend and asking him, "What does it mean if he waited four days after our date to text me?" He'll tell you the truth (whether you want to hear it or not).

**The work friend:** Okay, as much as you should never be best friends with someone you work with (see previous chapter), it's actually really nice to have someone at work to grab lunch with every day and know that they have your back. So while you don't need a WBF (work best friend), you can have a work friend.

**The more successful friend:** They say you are who you surround yourself with, and in that case it's good to have successful friends, because they will push you to be your better, more successful self. If you do have a successful friend, think about hosting a dinner with other successful ladies so the two of you can grow your network together.

**The "firsts" friend:** Everyone needs a friend who's gone through the firsts of life quickly. You know this girl. She was the first friend to have a serious boyfriend. The first friend to move in with the serious boyfriend. The first friend to marry the serious boyfriend. You need to be friends with someone who's been through life's milestones so you have someone to talk to when you're going through them yourself.

**The old friend:** Not to be confused with the older friend, the old friend is someone who's known you a long time. You guys start out every conversation with "Remember when . . ." Even if you and this friend have grown apart (it happens), your memories will always be there, and there's something special about having a friend who's seen you grow into the person you are.

**The friend who lives somewhere cool:** Try being friends with someone who lives somewhere you really like visiting, and you'll always have a place to crash when you want a vacation.

Got those friends? Good. Now turn to the next page and plan to invite them over for a dinner party.

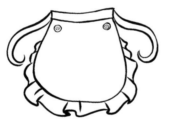

# So You're a Beginner at Dinner:
## Meals and Other Activities for Your First Dinner Party

> "I'm cooking us a dinner tonight at my place. It's going to be romantic and intimate and feature potatoes because I got a bag of 'em in my apartment that are about to go bad."
>
> Gabi Diamond, *Young & Hungry*

Throwing your first dinner party is a big deal. A dinner party tells the world that you are sophisticated, grown-up, and have enough room to host more than two people in your apartment (that alone should be celebrated). A dinner party does not need to be expensive and extravagant, where you break out the good china (or plastic). You *can* throw the dinner party of the century without having to break the bank. Even better? It's going to be fun. So get ready to throw the most fabulous dinner party of the year.

**STEP ONE—Why are you throwing this party?** Is this a dinner party in celebration of your kick-ass new job? Or maybe it's just a party celebrating the return of your favorite show, *Young & Hungry*. Whatever it is, before you send out your Evites, figure out the theme.

STEP TWO—**Who are you inviting?** The ideal size for a dinner party is between four and ten people. Choose your invite list wisely. Is this a party for single people or couples? Remember, no one likes to be the only single person at a couples' dinner. If you have a single friend you really want to invite to a couples' dinner, make sure to tell the friend ahead of time if he or she's going to be the lone ranger. Another question: how should you send out your invites? Evite, Paperless Post, Facebook events, and even just plain old e-mail all work. If you're really on it, try sending out your invites three weeks in advance. But don't sweat it; two weeks' notice is still plenty of time.

STEP THREE—**Plan your outfit:** You're the host of a magnificent dinner party and you need to look good. Choose something that's comfortable (so you can cook in it) but also festive. Red is celebratory and makes you stand out . . . and it will trigger your guests' appetites.

STEP FOUR—**Clean the bathroom:** There's nothing grosser than going to someone's house and seeing a dirty bathroom. And don't forget to make sure there's enough toilet paper. For the love of god, do not hand anyone a Kleenex box because that's all you have.

STEP FIVE—**Make a playlist:** Make a playlist that you and your crew will love. If your group is chatty, maybe stick to more mellow music like Beach House or Washed Out.

**STEP SIX—Booze:** You know what makes a dinner party great? Conversation? Yeah, right. Booze! Great booze will send your dinner party over the edge. You can add vodka to the strawberry basil lemonade recipe for a good party drink, but make sure that you've got some booze ready to drink straight up. Moscow Mules are great cocktails because they're easy: just vodka, ginger beer, and half a lime, and you're good to go. Pro tip: if your friends bring wine, don't feel like you absolutely *have* to drink it that night.

**STEP SEVEN—Decorate:** Nothing says *dinner party* more than cocktail napkins and candles. Now they don't need to be the crazy expensive candles; they can be from the drugstore. They just need to smell good and give the room some warmth.

**STEP EIGHT—Cook:** The final, but most important, step in your dinner party preparation is cooking dinner. Appetizers are essential:

- Mixed nuts
- Water crackers
- Brie cheese
- Olives
- Grapes
- Vegetables and dip
- Premade appetizers

It's a good idea to cook a practice round of your meal the week before just so you know that you can do it. What should you make? Gabi's magical one-pot spaghetti is an excellent option. Why? Not only is it easy, but everyone likes spaghetti. And, with some minor adjustments to the recipe, it can be made vegan or vegetarian. Also, if you invite someone who's gluten-free, there are plenty of gluten-free pasta options. So cook yourself some spaghetti and get ready for your impressive and utterly mature dinner party, you big adult, you!

# Magical One-Pot Spaghetti

Prep Time: 10 minutes       Cook Time: 55 minutes       Serves: 4–6

## Ingredients

- **1** tablespoon extra-virgin olive oil
- **1** pound lean ground beef (look for beef labeled 85/15)
- **1** yellow onion, peeled and chopped
- **2** garlic cloves, chopped
- **1** 8-ounce can crushed tomatoes
- **1** 6-ounce can tomato paste
- **3** cups tomato juice or tomato-based vegetable juice, like V8
- **1** cup water

- **1** teaspoon salt
- **2** teaspoons chili powder
- **1** teaspoon dried oregano
- **1** teaspoon dried basil
- **½** teaspoon ground black pepper
- **12** ounces spaghetti or fettuccine, uncooked
- Parmesan, grated
- Fresh parsley or basil, chopped, to garnish

## Directions

1. Heat the olive oil over medium-high heat in a large pot or Dutch oven, and add the beef, onion, and garlic.
2. Let cook for 2–3 minutes, then stir until beef crumbles and is no longer pink.
3. Stir in the crushed tomatoes, tomato paste, tomato juice, water, salt, chili powder, oregano, basil, and pepper.
4. Bring the mixture to a boil.
5. Cover, reduce heat, and simmer, stirring often, for 30 minutes.
6. Add the pasta and cover.
7. Let simmer, stirring often, for 20 minutes, or until pasta is tender.
8. Serve with the grated cheese and fresh herbs.

# Hosting Friendsgiving When You Don't Make a Good Living:
## Your Guide to a Cheap, Fun Holiday

Not everyone spends Thanksgiving with family. You might be far from home and have just spent a ton on tickets to go home for Christmas. You might only get two days off for Thanksgiving and have a work schedule that is kinda crazy. Or maybe you planned to go home but there was a huge snowstorm, and suddenly going home for Thanksgiving just doesn't seem possible. Don't be sad. Instead, find a group of friends who are also not going home for the holiday and invite them over for a little Friendsgiving.

Here's how to do it:

## For Food:

- **Buy a turkey:** How big of a bird should you buy? Well, the standard rule is one pound of turkey per person.
- **Ask each of your friends to bring a dish:** Everyone can bring something special. Maybe your friend Katie makes killer mashed potatoes. Perhaps Emily makes apple pie. Send out an e-mail with exactly what you need and ask each friend to come bearing their own dish. Here's how to divide things up:
  - **Turkey (you're bringing this):** Also buy some canned cranberry sauce and don't forget about the gravy.
  - **Drinks:** First of all, you've got to have some apple cider. But put two friends who can't cook in charge of bringing the alcohol.
  - **Appetizers (cheese and crackers, vegetables and dip):** Appetizers are also a good assignment for a friend who's not a real whiz in the kitchen.

- **Salad:** A salad can be simple and assigned to someone who doesn't cook. Or you can let a friend with real culinary skills bring a fancy, showstopping salad.
- **Sweet potatoes, mashed potatoes, stuffing, and other sides:** Assign to your friends who like to cook. For additional sides, brussels sprouts, roasted vegetables, corn bread, applesauce, and butternut squash are all excellent options.
- **Apple pie, pumpkin pie, and dessert:** Assign to your friends who like to bake.

Be mindful of people who are vegetarian or gluten-free. In addition to many traditional sides, mac 'n' cheese is a popular (not to mention extremely delicious) Thanksgiving dish for vegetarians.

## For Ambience:

- **Clean your place:** This should be obvious, but a few days before you host Friendsgiving, make sure that your apartment is clean and ready for guests.
- **Set a nice table:** Don't be embarrassed about going to Party City or shopping on Amazon.com for some Thanksgiving-themed decorations. They may be corny, but they'll also probably remind you of home. Don't want to buy anything? Some fall leaves sprinkled around your apartment can look pretty. And if you don't think you have enough silverware, just ask people to bring some.
- **Have a "thankful" jar:** Thanksgiving is all about being grateful for all the positive things in your life. To make your Friendsgiving even more special, have your guests write down what they're thankful for and

put the messages in a jar. At the end of the night, have every guest pick a random message out of the jar and read it out loud. This party game will bring your guests closer together.

- **Make a sweet playlist:** And since this is an American holiday, playing some classic American artists like Bruce Springsteen, the Beach Boys, and Taylor Swift will set the mood.

# Perfect Turkey

Prep Time: 10 minutes     Cook Time: Varies

## Ingredients

**1** thawed turkey (figure 1 pound per person—this includes bone weight). If you are expecting a small group (fewer than six), consider just cooking a turkey breast or a couple of whole chickens.

Salt and pepper

**1** cup unsalted melted butter or olive oil, divided

**2** cups chicken broth, turkey broth, white wine, or water

## Directions

### To cook the turkey:

1. Position an oven rack in the bottom third of your oven and preheat the oven to 450°F.

2. Rub the turkey all over with salt and pepper and arrange it breast up in a large roasting pan. (Don't worry about trussing or stuffing the turkey.)

3. Rub the turkey all over with half the butter or oil.

4. Pour the broth, wine, or water into the bottom of the roasting pan. (This will keep the meat moist as it roasts, and if you use broth or wine, it will enhance the flavor of the turkey juices.)

5. Put the turkey in the oven, on the lowest rack, and immediately turn the heat down to 350°F.

6. Roast the turkey for 13 minutes per pound, basting every 45 minutes (this just means brushing the turkey all over with the liquid from the bottom of the pan). You can use a turkey baster, a pastry brush, or even a small ladle.

(continues)

7. During the last 45 minutes of baking, baste the turkey 2–3 times with the remaining butter or oil (this will help turn the skin really golden brown and crispy).

8. Let the cooked turkey rest for at least 20 minutes before carving it.

9. Save the drippings—you can use them to make gravy later.

## To carve the turkey:

1. Get a sharp straight-edge slicing knife and a large carving fork (or a regular fork that is on the large side).

2. Place the turkey on a carving board with lipped edges, to catch the juices.

3. Beginning halfway up the breast, slice straight down.

4. When the knife reaches the space just above the wing joint, the slice should fall free on its own.

5. Continue to slice breast meat, starting the cut at a higher point each time. Repeat until the whole breast is sliced.

6. Transfer the slices to a serving platter.

7. Grasp the end of the drumstick, place your knife between the drumstick and the body of the turkey, and cut straight through the skin to the joint (if your knife is sharp, it should go right through).

8. Remove the entire leg by pulling out and back, using the sharp tip of the knife to slice through it. Separate the thigh and drumstick at the joint, set them on the serving platter, and repeat with the remaining thigh and drumstick.

9. Insert a fork in the upper wing to steady the turkey.

10. Make a long horizontal cut above the wing joint through the body frame.

11. Remove the wing, add it to the serving platter, and repeat with the second wing.

# Homemade Gravy

Prep Time: 2 minutes    Cook Time: 10 minutes    Makes: about 2 cups of gravy

## Ingredients

¼  cup butter

¼  cup flour

4  cups turkey drippings (the stuff in the bottom of the pan after you cook the turkey)

Salt and pepper, to taste

## Directions

1. Melt butter over medium-high heat in a medium saucepan. Whisk in flour and cook, whisking constantly, until it begins to turn light brown.

2. Whisk in the turkey drippings in 1-cup increments.

3. Bring to a boil, reduce to a simmer, and cook, whisking frequently, until the gravy is thick and creamy. This should take about 10 minutes.

4. Remove from heat and add salt and pepper if it needs it (it likely won't, as the drippings are already pretty salty, but it's good to check).

Now that you've celebrated your first Friendsgiving and are truly happy (and thankful) for your apartment, your job, your healthy body, and your friends, you might be ready for some love in your life. This next chapter is all about the thing that people have been writing about for centuries . . . love.

# 5

# Swipe Rights and Yummy Bites

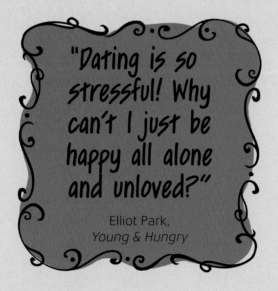

"Dating is so stressful! Why can't I just be happy all alone and unloved?"

Elliot Park,
*Young & Hungry*

# Introduction

Finding love today is at once easier (your next date is just one swipe away) and harder than ever. (Juliet never had to worry about not getting a text back from Romeo). The hardest thing about love in the modern age is that not only do you have so many options and so many ways to communicate (Snapchat, Facebook, texts, Google chat), but you're inundated with information, which often makes dating much more complicated. What does it mean when a guy you have a crush on sends you a funny Snapchat? What does it mean if he refuses to put a photo of the two of you on Instagram? Dating in the digital age has its own set of problems, but there are certain strategies and recipes that'll help you through it. From helping you get over your first big breakup, to finding love abroad, to dating apps, and—eventually—how to navigate being in a relationship, this chapter is going to set you up to get whisked away by love.

# Nacho Boyfriend Anymore:
## How to Get Over a Breakup (Nacho Recipe Included)

"Everything happens for a reason. Maybe it didn't work out because there's something better out there."

Josh Kaminski, *Young & Hungry*

You fell in love and then something awful happened . . . it ended. Maybe you were the one who got dumped. Maybe you were the one who decided to end things. Maybe you were ghosted—which feels worse than being dumped. For those unfamiliar with the term *ghosting*, it means a guy just disappears. You're dating, you think everything's going well, and then suddenly . . . he stops texting. Even if he's straightforward, it's incredibly hard to go from hearing "I love you" to "We need to talk."

Unless you marry the first person you ever date (which happens, and to those women out there, we're all jealous), you, like most women, are going to have to kiss a lot of toads before you find your Prince Charming. And if that's the case, you're going to have to go through your fair share of breakups. Here are our best tips for getting over a breakup.

**Cleanse your apartment:** When Gabi and Josh broke up, she boxed up the stuff of his that she still had. As Gabi told Sofia, "I'm de-Kaminski-ing our apartment. Anything Josh has ever given to me I'm throwing away." How do

you do the same thing? For starters, get rid of pictures that remind you of your ex, the stuffed animals he won for you, the Dodgers hat from your first game together, etc. Now, you don't have to burn his stuff. In fact, if things ended amicably, put the items in a bag and send his stuff to him. The most important thing is that you have a fresh start with all your ex's stuff out of the way.

**Stop following him on social media:** Seriously, you do not need to look at pictures of your ex and his new girlfriend. So stop following him on Instagram and looking at his Snapchat stories. As Sofia once said, "The whole point of Instagram is to make everyone think you're happier than they are." Who knows if the photos of your ex are real or staged? It's not worth looking at!

**Cry:** It's important that you mourn the loss of a relationship. If you think you need some additional support, try to find a licensed therapist in your area.

**Have a fun weekend with your girlfriends:** Getting dumped is horrible, but it does mean one good thing . . . girls' night! If you've experienced a breakup, the best thing to do is go out for a night on the town. And remember, you're not looking to meet someone, you're just looking to have fun. In fact, you shouldn't even be looking *at* guys. If you're looking, you'll get to the bar, glance around, turn to your friends, and say, "(Insert ex's name here) is so much cuter than every guy in this place." And the next thing you know you're crying hysterically in the bathroom as your friends hold your phone so you can't text the ex. Don't do this. Just be prepared to dance and drink, and have an old-fashioned sleepover with your girls.

**Don't text your ex:** Texting your ex gets you nowhere. You don't want to get back with him. You broke up for a reason. If you really think you can't stop yourself from drunk-dialing or tipsy-texting, delete his number from your phone so you're not even tempted. Or go into your contacts and change his contact name to DO NOT TEXT THIS GUY.

**Make out with a new guy:** Some people say you have to sleep with someone new, but the truth is making out with a new guy can do the trick. There's just something fun about meeting a stranger at a bar, letting him buy you a drink, and at the end of the night, giving him a little kiss before you and your girls hop into an Uber.

**When you're ready, go out with the guy you passed up before:** Every girl has this guy. The guy you had such great chemistry with but never let yourself date because you had a boyfriend. Guess what? You don't have a boyfriend anymore, which means you are free to date. Send this guy a text— JUST WANTED TO LET YOU KNOW . . . I'M SINGLE—and see what he does. If he makes a move . . . you just got your next date.

**Get back on the apps:** The best part of online dating is that it's so easy to find your next date. Download Bumble, Tinder, Hinge, The League, Coffee Meets Bagel, etc., and be prepared to get back out there. Start out with either Coffee Meets Bagel or The League, because both of these apps only send you a limited number of people a day (between two and eight) and it might be too overwhelming to get on Tinder if you haven't dated in years.

**Make a list:** This may sound crazy, but failed relationships can be beneficial. You know why? Every failed relationship leads you closer and closer to finding the guy you're meant to be with. After you end your relationship, make a list of qualities that you liked about your ex. Whether it was his sense of humor, his height, or his religion, something drew you to this guy in the first place. Then, in another document, make a list of qualities that you need but didn't get from this guy. Maybe you need a guy who's as ambitious as you are. Maybe you're a vegan and it really bothered you when your last guy ate ribs. Every girl has something different that she needs out of a relationship, and it's really important for you to know what you need going forward.

**Make some nachos:** Breakup calories don't count. You're allowed one total pig-out weekend where you can eat your feelings. In honor of eating your feelings, try this recipe for easy oven nachos.

# Easy Oven Nachos

Prep Time: 15 minutes     Cook Time: 12 minutes     Serves: 4

## Ingredients

**6** cups tortilla chips

**1** 15-ounce can pinto, black, or navy beans, rinsed
and drained

**3** cups cheddar or jack cheese, shredded

**1** 4-ounce can chopped green chilies, drained

**1** avocado, diced

**4** green onions, sliced

**1** 4-ounce can sliced olives, drained

**2** Roma tomatoes, cored and diced (or 1/2 cup cherry/
grape tomatoes, halved)

**½** cup sour cream (optional)

## Directions

1. Preheat oven to 375°F.

2. Spread chips over an ungreased baking sheet. Scatter beans over the chips.

3. Cover with shredded cheese and bake for 10–12 minutes, or until cheese is melted and bubbly.

4. Top baked nachos with green chilies, avocado, green onions, olives, tomatoes, and sour cream (if using).

5. Serve immediately.

# Friends with Benedicts:
## When to Cook Breakfast and Other Rules for Navigating a Friends-with-Benefits Situation

*"I hate it when guys want to talk and cuddle. It's like, I got needs, bitch!"*

Sofia Rodriguez,
*Young & Hungry*

Navigating a friends-with-benefits (or FWB for short) situation isn't easy, but at some point in your life you might enjoy the benefits of, well, a friend with benefits. However, benefiter beware: do not fall in love with this guy. You know how it goes. You have a crazy hot sex life with this person and suddenly you're overlooking the fact that he lives with his parents and has a man-bun.

So how do you know if you have a FWB candidate? Well, for starters:

- **He's not boyfriend material:** Now this can mean a lot of things. Maybe he's just emotionally unavailable. Maybe he's Jewish and you swore that you would marry a Catholic. Maybe his personality is just plain annoying. The biggest thing this guy has going for him is that . . .
- **You're sexually attracted:** Something about this guy just really turns you on. Sure, you hate that he talks about CrossFit all the damn time.

But when you're lying in bed next to him and he's working with a six-pack, you really like the fact that he does CrossFit.

- **He's respectful:** Do not get into a FWB situation if your guy is disrespectful in any way. This relationship should be entirely on your terms. *You* text him when you want him. If he texts you in the middle of the night, only respond when *you* want to. And respectful also means that he's cool using protection every time.

Now that you've found a guy to be your FWB, it's time to set up some ground rules.

- **Don't bring your FWB to a wedding or any public event as your date:** He's not your boyfriend. Don't treat him as such.
- **Don't text him about things other than where and when:** Otherwise he's taking up too much mental space that could be spent flirting with other guys.
- **Don't be jealous:** If you see your FWB out with another girl, do not be jealous. Remember that you signed up for this and he's not doing anything wrong by going out with this girl.
- **Don't see him more than once a week:** If you're hanging out with your FWB more than once a week, he kinda seems like your boyfriend. Keep this at a minimum. As Alan in *Young & Hungry* advises Gabi and Josh when they start their friends-with-benefits relationship, "You want to keep having sex, but you don't want to develop feelings for each other. So just stop the sex before you start having feelings."
- **Be really demanding about what you want in bed:** This guy is lucky enough to have sex with you without any sense of commitment, so be as demanding as you want. The key to a successful FWB relationship is making sure your needs are met.

- **No dinner dates:** Dinner is what couples do, and you are NOT a couple. There's only one meal you should be eating with your FWB, and that's breakfast. If he sleeps over (and is deserving of something yummy), then and only then are you allowed to make him breakfast. And since you two probably burned some serious sex calories, feel free to treat yourselves to some awesomely delicious eggs Benedict.

# Eggs Benedict with Avocado and Sriracha Hollandaise

Prep Time: 5 minutes　　Cook Time: 15 minutes　　Serves: 2

## Ingredients

**2** tablespoons unsalted butter

Juice of one lemon

**6** eggs, divided

¼ cup half-and-half

**2** teaspoons sriracha

Salt

½ teaspoon pepper

**2** tablespoons white vinegar

**2** English muffins or 4 pieces of bread

**1** avocado, sliced

## Directions

1. To make the hollandaise sauce, create a double boiler by placing a heatproof bowl over a small pot of water.

2. Bring the water to a light boil over high heat and add the butter to the bowl.

3. Allow it to slowly melt.

4. Reduce the heat to medium and add the lemon juice and the yolks of 2 of the eggs.

5. Whisk gently until the mixture begins to thicken.

6. Slowly add the half-and-half until the consistency is rich and creamy.

7. Season with the sriracha, ¼ teaspoon salt, and the pepper. Remove from heat.

(continues)

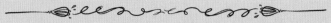

8. Halve and toast the English muffins or bread slices.

9. While they toast, fill a 12-inch nonstick pan with water. Cover, and bring to a boil. Stir in 1 teaspoon salt and the white vinegar.

10. Reduce the heat to a simmer.

11. Crack each of the remaining 4 eggs into its own small bowl or cup.

12. Gently pour each egg into the simmering water, doing your best to keep a little space between each one so they don't fuse.

13. Turn off the heat, cover the pan, and let the eggs cook for 5 minutes (longer if you want a yolk that is fully cooked). Don't poke or check the eggs while they poach!

14. While the eggs are cooking, remove the toasted English muffins or bread from the toaster or oven and top with the sliced avocado.

15. Top each muffin half or toast slice with a poached egg and a drizzle of the hollandaise sauce.

16. Serve hot.

# French Dishes and French Kisses:
## How to Find Romance Abroad

Ah, the international romance. The best thing about having a lover abroad is that you never have to see this person again if you don't want to—mainly because he lives thousands of miles away. The chances of your running into Roberto from Milan at your local 7-Eleven are slim to none. But how does one have a romance abroad? Let's break it down.

**Choose where you want to go (and don't break the bank):** Maybe you read *Eat, Pray, Love* and have been dreaming of going on a trip to Italy, India, and Indonesia. Or maybe you've had this fantasy of falling in love with an Australian guy because you're obsessed with the Hemsworth brothers. The first step in having a romance abroad is picking the right location. As for getting deals, try the following:

- **Use Kayak.com (or other comparison sites):** This is one way to make sure you get the best deal on your flights.
- **Book midweek:** Airline tickets are usually cheaper when you purchase them during the week than on the weekend.
- **Confirm your dates:** Switching flights can be really expensive, so be as sure of your travel dates as possible before booking.
- **Leave on a Wednesday:** Statistically, Wednesday is the cheapest day to embark.
- **Fly out at the crack of dawn:** The earlier the flight, the cheaper it usually is.

**You've landed! Now head to your hotel (or hostel):** Ask whoever is working there where the local hot spot is. Go there looking your best. Have some fun flirting and enjoying the freedom of knowing you'll never see these people again in your life. But be smart and cautious; don't let a sexy accent seduce you into doing something you'll regret.

**Another suggestion:** When you're at a bar, a café, a museum, or a park, go up to the cutest guy you see and tell him you're American. Ask for advice on the best local places to visit.

**Remove your "abroad" glasses:** Take off your "I'm in Paris, every guy's cute" glasses and really look at this guy. If this exact same guy walked into a bar in Denver, would you still want to jump his bones? If the answer is no, then he's not worthy of being your hookup abroad.

**Don't get in this for the conversation:** If you don't speak the language, there's going to be a huge barrier, and you just need to be aware of your limitations. Your relationship abroad might be hot, but the conversation could be lacking. If the only question you can ask in Spanish is "What's your favorite color?" things aren't going to get very deep.

**Take pics so you'll always remember your hot romance abroad:** If your Italian dude is smoking hot, take pictures of the two of you together so that one day, when you're married to Paul from Cleveland, you'll remember your single days and the sexy romance you and Mario had in Tuscany.

**More than romance:** The best part about traveling to foreign places is that it builds confidence and opens your mind to new people and cultures. So, when you're not meeting men, what types of things should you do when traveling abroad? Here are some suggestions for some epic single-lady adventures:

- **Take public transportation:** The best way to get to know a new city is to take public transportation.

Whether it's the bus in Istanbul or the Tube in London, public transportation is a great way to see the area and get a feel for the different neighborhoods.

- **Go to live events:** Every city has live events specific to its history and culture. Maybe you go to Venice for Carnival, or maybe you take tango lessons in Argentina. Wherever you're traveling, make a point of attending unique celebrations.

- **Shop at the smaller stores:** Local businesses and family-owned places will give you a clearer picture of the area. Also, spots geared toward tourists are often overpriced.

- **Take a tour:** Some cities even offer free tours. For example, if you stay at a hostel, there are sometimes free walking tours led by college students. Or you might hire an inexpensive local tour guide to take you around and show you the hottest spots.

- **Have a plan, but allow yourself to deviate:** Many travelers become obsessed with sticking to an itinerary. Having an idea of where you want to go is helpful, but allow yourself the time and freedom to wander off and explore little coffee shops or bookstores that might not have been on your list.

- **Protect your memories:** You're going to want to remember this trip for the rest of your life. Make sure to buy little souvenirs from the different places you visit. They don't have to be expensive. In fact, the best way to remember a good trip is to cook food from the place you visited. And while there are many amazing dishes from different countries, there's nothing quite like a croissant. Whether you've been to France or just love delicious croissants, make this recipe, and get ready for a true French adventure.

# Easy Chocolate Croissants

Prep Time: 10 minutes     Cook Time: 15–20 minutes     Makes: 8 croissants

## Ingredients

**1** 8-ounce can of refrigerated crescent rolls

**²/₃** cup chopped chocolate or chocolate chips (milk chocolate or semisweet chocolate)

Powdered sugar (optional), for garnish

## Directions

1. Preheat the oven to 350°F.

2. Line a baking sheet with parchment paper (or grease with nonstick cooking spray).

3. Separate the dough into 8 triangles by pulling it apart at the seams.

4. Place a tablespoon of chocolate onto the wide end of each triangle.

5. Roll up, starting with the wide end of the triangle and rolling to the opposite point. Pull the ends in to form a crescent shape.

6. Arrange the croissants on the prepared baking sheet.

7. Bake at 350°F for 15–20 minutes or until golden brown. Sprinkle with powdered sugar.

# Taco 'bout Online Dating:
## You Can Make the Perfect Taco and the Perfect Date in Twenty Minutes

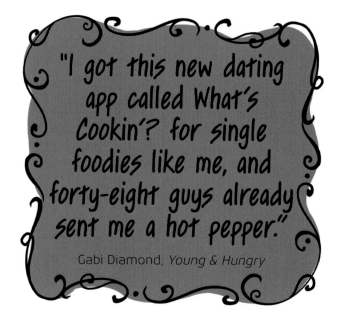

"I got this new dating app called What's Cookin'? for single foodies like me, and forty-eight guys already sent me a hot pepper."

Gabi Diamond, *Young & Hungry*

In twenty minutes you can find your husband. Okay, maybe not your husband. But you can find someone to go out with this Friday night. How? Easy: online dating.

The great thing about dating online is that it's like going to a bar, except you can still hang out in your pajamas. You can literally wake up before work, hang out in bed, grab your phone, and start looking for hot prospects. And online dating doesn't have the stigma it once had. In *Young & Hungry*, Gabi, Sofia, and Yolanda are all dating online. In fact, Gabi even went on a dating app specific to foodies. There are all kinds of dating apps that you can take advantage of, and this chapter is going to lay out the most popular dating apps and their pros and cons. Here's how you find the perfect online date in twenty minutes *while* making yourself some delicious tacos.

MINUTE 1: **Think about what you want.** Did you recently get out of a long-term relationship and are just looking for a good time? Or maybe you're ready for the real deal. Knowing what you want will help you pick the right app and the right person.

MINUTE 2: **Download the apps.** Here's a quick guide to some popular dating apps.

- **Tinder:** Tinder has a reputation for hookups, but plenty of people use it to find love. Tinder supposedly has fifty million users, which gives people like you *lots* of options. The downside? You're inundated with people every time you log in, which could be overwhelming if you're new to online dating.

- **Hinge:** This is a great dating app because it only links you to people you are friends with or friends of friends with (using Facebook to do so). In this case, your date knows that you have friends in common, so he's probably less likely to act like a jerk.

- **Bumble:** Bumble is like Tinder in the sense that you're inundated with tons of people. But there's a catch: girls have to message the guys first, and they have twenty-four hours to do so. After that, the match is deleted.

- **Coffee Meets Bagel:** The pro of this app is that it only gives you a limited number of matches, which is comforting when you're first dipping your toe in the online dating pond. This site also has a time constraint. You have eight days to start chatting with your match, or they are deleted from your search.

- **The League:** This app is for people who are into education. It originally started for people who only wanted to date Ivy League graduates, but it soon morphed to include other people who are educated and have good jobs. However, this app doesn't accept everyone who applies, so don't be upset if you get rejected.
- **Raya:** Raya is a dating app specifically for people who work in creative industries. This app is not for people afraid of rejection, since Raya is also an app that doesn't accept everyone who applies. You need a referral to get in *plus* a healthy Instagram presence.
- **Jswipe, Collide, Minder:** These dating apps are specific to religious groups: Jews, Christians, and Muslims, respectively. This type of dating app works well when you want to date someone of the same religion.

MINUTE 3: **Upload your profile pictures.** Here's some unexpected advice: do not choose your absolute best photos. Of course, choose photos that are flattering and highlight your favorite features, but don't make your photos so insanely beautiful that your date will be disappointed when he meets you. When you go on dates, you want to be the pleasant surprise and not the disappointment. You want guys to say, "Wow, you are so much cuter in person." Those guys will ask you out again! They wanted to meet you already, but now that they see how cool you are as a person and that you're *even cuter* than you were online, they will practically melt in your arms. You may have friends with professional photos that are Photoshopped to make them look skinnier and prettier, but these girls are hiding behind a facade. Show your true self and watch as you become the envy of all your friends.

MINUTES 4–5: **Write your profile.** Keep your info to a minimum, and don't say exactly what you're looking for. Nothing turns guys off more than a girl writing, *I'm looking for a tall successful guy who's close with his mom and doesn't mind coming to spin class with me on Sundays*. Instead, give your occupation and where you grew up. For example, *New York girl living in Los Angeles writing for TV.* It's simple. It gives the guy good conversational jumping-off points (e.g., *"Hey, New Yawker"*) and it doesn't say too much.

MINUTES 6–7: **Start swiping.** Don't be judgy. Err on the side of swiping right more often than not. Guys do this. A lot of guys will swipe right on almost every girl and then see who likes *them*. Ladies, this is a great strategy. Okay, so he doesn't look like the tallest guy in his pictures, but what if he messages you and he's so funny that you forget he's five foot seven? Be more open-minded and it will pay off.

MINUTE 8: **Check out your matches.** Now that you're swiping right more often than not, you've probably got some good matches. If there's anyone that you're really truly not excited about, feel free to delete him. You don't want your Tinder inbox crowded with guys who don't have a chance with you.

MINUTES 9–10: **Start responding.** Before you start writing to guys (which is totally acceptable, 'cause this is the modern world), see who messages you. If there are guys who are cute and interesting, respond to their messages. If they don't immediately ask a question (or if their message is something vague like "Hey, lady"), then feel free to ask them a little something like, "Hello, sir. How's your day going?"

MINUTE 11: **Engage in the textual banter.** Banter is fun. It lets you see if you and the guy have some chemistry. But beware: some guys are funny over text but kind of boring and quiet in person. The guy who killed it with the zingers over text is sometimes the most awkward person you've ever met in real life.

MINUTE 12: **Juggle some dudes.** Don't just talk to one guy, but don't talk to a hundred guys at once. Talking to five guys is probably enough that you won't get bored, but is easy enough to juggle.

MINUTE 13: **Know the basics.** Before you go out with a guy, you should know the following information:

- What he does for a living (and if he *has* a living)
- Where he's from
- Where he's currently residing (ideally not on the street)

MINUTE 14: **Give him time to ask you out.** But if a guy does not ask you out for an in-person date within two days of messaging, stop talking to him. If he writes to ask you what happened, tell the dude that you're not looking for a pen pal—you're looking to meet up with people in person.

MINUTE 15: **Be aware of any red flags.** One such red flag is if he asks you out for that night. Any guy that ever utters the five words "What are you doing tonight?" during your first conversation is not looking for a relationship . . . he's looking to get some.

MINUTE 16: **If choosing between two guys to go out with, choose the safer guy first.** When you're just getting your feet wet in online dating, you'll be flooded with dates. As tempting as it is to make your first date the guy with the six-pack, try choosing someone whom you have something in common with. Why? If the sparks aren't there, you'll probably still have a stimulating conversation.

MINUTE 17: **Do some light stalking.** Before you start dating a guy you met online, it makes sense to investigate. You might come across some crucial information, such as the fact that he has a girlfriend . . . whom he is living with! A quick Google or Facebook search can ensure you don't go out with anyone creepy. And if he's not on Facebook? Well, as Sofia in *Young & Hungry* tells Gabi when they can't find her date on Facebook, "You know who's not on Facebook? Criminals, hoodlums, and my aunt Becky who lives in the forest." Remember that, ladies!

MINUTE 18: **Coordinate a date.** Okay, so the guy you thought was cute asked you out! Now, remember, don't cancel anything with your girlfriends just because that's the only time he's available. You do not want to miss the Justin Bieber concert with your friends for what ends up being a disappointing date.

MINUTE 19: **Pick somewhere neutral.** A guy might think he's being chivalrous, but don't let someone you don't know pick you up at your apartment. It's a little creepy, and you don't want anyone you don't know to know where you live.

MINUTE 20: **Give yourself one full minute to get excited.** You're going on a date! Now keep in mind this one important fact: it's a numbers game! This is your first date out of many. You might go on forty-three online dates in one year before you find your boyfriend. It might take you forty-four. It might take you five. But when you find the right person, it'll be like the perfect taco. Just as tacos combine meat and toppings into one delicious meal, you are combining people and personalities into one filling, satisfying relationship. Now get out there—and start cooking some chipotle chicken tacos.

# Chipotle Chicken Tacos

Prep Time: 20 minutes     Cook Time: 10 minutes     Serves: 3–4

## Ingredients

**1** pound boneless, skinless chicken thighs, chopped into 1-inch pieces

**2** chipotle peppers from a can packed in adobo, diced finely, plus 2 tablespoons of the adobo sauce

Salt and pepper

**1** tablespoon extra-virgin olive oil

**½** medium red onion, chopped finely, divided

**3** cloves garlic, chopped

**1** mango, chopped into ¼-inch pieces

**1** Roma tomato, seeded and chopped

**1** handful fresh cilantro leaves, chopped finely

Juice of ½ lime

**6-8** corn tortillas

## Directions

1. Combine the chicken with the peppers, sauce, and ½ teaspoon each of salt and pepper in a mixing bowl.

2. Mix well using clean hands or a spoon, making sure each piece of chicken is well coated. Set aside.

3. Heat the olive oil in a large frying pan over medium-high heat. Add half the sliced onion and the garlic and cook for 1 minute, stirring occasionally.

4. Add chicken and cook for 7–8 minutes, stirring occasionally.

5. Check a piece of chicken to make sure it's fully cooked. Turn heat down to low to keep chicken mixture warm.

(continues)

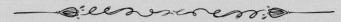

6. Toss together the remaining diced onion, mango, tomato, cilantro leaves, and lime juice, and salt and pepper to taste. Set aside.

7. Heat a dry grill pan or large frying pan over high heat and lightly grill the tortillas on each side. Remove from heat and set aside.

8. To assemble tacos, place about ¼ cup chicken mixture in a tortilla and top with the fresh mango salsa. Serve immediately.

**HINT:** Leftovers work well as a brown-bag lunch. Simply wrap a few tortillas in foil and pack some of the chicken mixture in a thermos or other heat-safe container and assemble your tacos on the go.

# The Exclusive Conversation:
## It's Not Easy, but This Trifle Recipe Is

Congratulations! You met someone and you want it to be exclusive. That's hard to do, especially when you're on dating apps and have so many options. But there's just something about this guy that keeps you coming back for more. Maybe it's the fact that he's so fun and easy to talk to. Or maybe you want to sleep with this guy and you're not willing to do that unless you're in an exclusive relationship.

A lot of guys are reluctant to broach the subject of monogamy. It's not necessarily a bad thing—just a guy thing. They might not even be seeing other girls. Many guys just don't understand the point of bringing it up. Sometimes guys assume that you are exclusive without having the conversation. However, if you are the kind of girl who wants to get everything out on the table, it's important to talk about exclusivity.

One piece of advice: do not have the *exclusive* conversation after two dates. That will make you seem crazy. The appropriate time to have this conversation is right around six dates (or after about one month of dating).

But the real question is how you even know when you're heading toward exclusivity. Here are some signs that say you two are probably only seeing each other.

- **You've met his friends:** Guys don't introduce just any random girl to their buddies. If you've met his friends, he's showing you off (and getting the approval of his dudes). But remember, ladies: just because you've met his roommate doesn't mean you're getting married.
- **You're hanging out on Saturdays:** Most guys don't like giving up their weekends for new girls. But if a guy is making it a priority to see you over the weekend, chances are he's serious about you.

- **You're leaving stuff at each other's place:** If you are leaving stuff at a guy's place, and he's leaving stuff at your place, it's a sign that you two are spending a lot of time together and heading in a serious direction.
- **You're making plans weeks in advance:** Suddenly, your guy is talking about taking you to a concert next month. Or he's floated the idea of you two taking a vacation together this summer (and it's December). When someone is talking about the future, they also probably want to be dating exclusively.

So now that you're pretty sure you are exclusive (or heading there), here's how to approach the conversation.

- Keep in mind this is *not* a conversation you should be having over text, no matter how old you are. Please never text a guy with HEY, YOU WANNA BE MY BOYFRIEND? or WHERE IS THIS GOING? The *exclusive* talk has to happen in person, and there's simply no other way to do it.
- If you haven't slept with the guy yet, you can say, "I don't usually sleep with someone unless we're dating exclusively." Now the guy has two responses. He can either say, "I'm not ready to be in a relationship," or he can say, "Well, that's sweet, because I want to be your boyfriend. Can we bone now?"
- Wait until an event. Let's say your company Christmas party is coming up and your guy has agreed to go with you. One easy way of starting the relationship conversation is saying, "Hey, I'm so happy you're coming to the Christmas party with me, but how do you think I should introduce you?"
- If you can't wait until an event and you've already slept with him, here's what to do. The next time you're on a date, simply say, "I'm having a

lot of fun, and I don't want to date anyone else." This is a nice way of saying, "I'm not dating anyone else, so neither should you." It also gives him an opportunity to voice his thoughts. He could say, "I still want to date around. . . ." But he could also say, "I don't want to date anyone else, either." Just like that . . . you're exclusive.

What do you do next? Make you and your boo some berry trifle, change your relationship status on Facebook from *single* to *in a relationship*, and celebrate the fact that you had the talk. See? It wasn't so bad!

# Easy Berry Trifle

Prep Time: 5 hours (includes refrigeration)   Cook Time: 6 minutes   Serves: 2

## Ingredients

### For the pudding:

2¼ cups milk (preferably whole, but 2% or even coconut milk would work), divided

½ cup sugar

⅙ cup cornstarch

¼ teaspoon salt

3 large egg yolks, lightly beaten with a fork

1 teaspoon vanilla extract

OR

Prepare 1 box vanilla pudding mix according to directions.

### For the trifle:

½ 8-inch store-bought vanilla pound cake, sliced into ½-inch cubes

½ pint sliced fresh strawberries or fresh raspberries (or use a mixture)

1 cup whipped cream (canned is fine)

## Directions

### To make the pudding:

1. Heat 2 cups milk in a large saucepan over medium heat until steaming.

2. Whisk the sugar, cornstarch, and salt in a large bowl.

3. Whisk in the egg yolks and the remaining ¼ cup milk.

(continues)

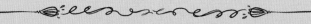

4. Whisk half of the hot milk into the egg mixture until smooth, then gradually whisk the egg-milk mixture into the saucepan. Cook over medium heat, whisking constantly, until the mixture boils. Continue to cook, whisking constantly, until it reaches a thick, creamy consistency (this should take 3–4 minutes).

5. Remove from heat and stir in the vanilla.

6. Cool slightly, stirring occasionally (to prevent a "skin" from forming).

7. Place a piece of plastic wrap directly on top of the pudding and refrigerate until completely cooled and thickened, about 4 hours.

8. Just before assembling the trifle, whisk the pudding until smooth and creamy.

## To make the trifle:

1. Put a layer of cake cubes on the bottom of a large wineglass or a pretty dessert bowl. Top with a layer of pudding and a layer of berries.

2. Top with a second layer of cake cubes, a second layer of pudding, and a second layer of berries.

3. Repeat with the remaining ingredients in a second glass.

4. Top each trifle with a generous serving of whipped cream and the remaining berries. Let chill for at least an hour before serving.

# Just the Two of Us:
## Things to Do Now That There Are Two

So, you put yourself out there. You went on the online dating apps. You forced yourself to go on dates with strangers. And then something happened: you met someone exciting. Someone who texted you at reasonable hours. Someone funny. Someone with whom you immediately felt a crazy strong connection. And then what happened? You started hanging out twice a week, then three times, and then before you knew it . . . you had a boyfriend! Being in a relationship with someone you love is one of the great joys in life. However, it's really easy to get into relationship ruts. Like when every Saturday night you're curled up in bed watching Netflix. Here are some ideas to spice up your Saturday nights.

## Great Date Ideas:

- **Arcade:** It's like a high school date, but this time you guys can order beer.
- **Go to a comedy show:** Not all comedy shows are created equal. Some of them might really suck. But go to one with your bae and try your hardest to laugh (even if it takes a couple of cocktails).
- **Go to an amusement park:** Head to your local Six Flags with your guy and ride some crazy roller coasters (and be thankful that your relationship isn't one . . . a roller coaster, that is).
- **Day trippin':** Make a killer playlist and then get in a car and head somewhere for the day. It doesn't need to be a well-known scene, but the experience of going somewhere for the first time together is all you really need.

- **Wine tasting:** Getting a little tipsy is fun and sexy. Go to one of your favorite bars and do some wine tasting. Lots of gourmet stores and wine bars organize wine tastings of their own.
- **Take me out to the ball game:** Order a hot dog and a beer, and watch the game (or each other).
- **Bowling:** The best thing about bowling? If you're terrible, you can ask your man to stand behind you and give you some lessons.
- **Outdoor movies:** In Los Angeles there's a thing called Cinespia, where they have outdoor screenings of movies in cemeteries (less creepy than it sounds). Pick up a pizza and find an outdoor movie screening or a drive-in near you.
- **Cook dinner together:** Cooking is such a great bonding activity because there's nothing like food to bring people together. Use our pizza party recipe and stay in for the night to cook this delicious meal.

# Pizza Party for Two

Prep Time: 15 minutes     Cook Time: 16–20 minutes     Serves: 2 (with leftovers)

## Ingredients

### For the Dough:

**1** cup warm water

**1** packet dry active yeast

**2** tablespoons sugar

**1** teaspoon salt

**2½** cups flour

**2** tablespoons olive oil, plus more for the bowl

OR

**1** pound store-bought pizza dough

### Sauces

Marinara

Pesto

Ranch dressing

Extra-virgin olive oil

### Cheeses

Mozzarella, shredded

Fresh buffalo mozzarella, torn into pieces

Cheddar, shredded

Jack, shredded

Goat cheese, crumbled

Feta, crumbled

### Toppings

Pepperoni or salami, sliced

Olives, sliced

Artichoke hearts

Fresh vegetables (red peppers, mushrooms, zucchini, spinach, kale, onions, etc.), sliced

Leftover cooked chicken, shredded or chopped

Garlic, chopped

Canned green chilies, chopped

(continues)

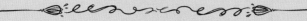

# Directions

## To make the dough from scratch:

1. Preheat the oven to 350°F, then turn it off as soon as it has preheated. This will allow the oven to be warm enough for when you make the dough.

2. Combine water, yeast, and sugar and set aside in a warm place until it begins to foam, about 4–5 minutes.

3. Meanwhile, in a mixing bowl, combine the salt and flour. Slowly pour in the yeast mixture and add the olive oil until a dough begins to form.

4. Knead the dough for 2–3 minutes.

5. Set dough aside in an oiled bowl, covered with a damp dish towel, in the warmed (make sure you turned it off!) oven for 30 minutes.

6. With a fist, gently punch down the dough in the bowl, and let it rest for 10 minutes.

## To make the pizzas:

1. Preheat the oven to 475°F.

2. Line 2 baking sheets with parchment paper (or lightly grease and sprinkle with flour).

3. Divide the dough into 4 pieces.

4. Stretch each round into an 8-inch circle (or any shape you like).

5. Place the dough round on the prepared baking sheet.

6. Top each dough round with ¼ cup of your favorite sauce, using the bottom of a spoon to spread it around. Make sure to leave a ½-inch border for the crust.

7. Top the sauce with 1 cup of your cheese of choice (or a combination of cheeses).

8. Add your toppings of choice. **HINT:** Don't overload the pizza with toppings! A too-heavy pizza will become gloppy and weighed-down in the oven and won't be fun to eat.

9. Bake the pizzas for 16–20 minutes, until the crust is golden brown and the cheese is bubbly and melted.

10. Slice into wedges and serve hot.

It's so nice being in love, but there are some hazards of being in a relationship that you should be aware of. Avoid potential danger by following this advice:

- **Don't forget about your friends:** It's so easy to forget about your friends when you have a new romance. When you're in a brand-new relationship, you're allowed six weeks to blow off your friends, but after that you need to come back down to planet Earth.

- **Never argue in front of people:** If you're mad at your partner for whatever reason, try your hardest not to get into a blowout fight in front of your friends. It won't make either of you look good. Keep the fighting private.

- **Respect each other's privacy:** It's so tempting to hack into your dude's phone, but when he trusts you with his iPhone so you can read him directions from Waze, seriously—do not go into his text messages and start reading. Everyone deserves privacy.

- **Don't take him for granted:** When you've been dating someone for a long time, it's easy to start taking him for granted. Try your hardest to remember what drew you to him in the first place.

- **Don't obsess over his exes:** Almost every girl is obsessed with stalking her boyfriend's ex-girlfriend. *Is she skinnier than I am? She's blond and I'm brunette. Oh god, does this mean he has a thing for blondes?* Stop obsessing about his ex-girlfriend and remember that there's a reason why he's not with her anymore—he's with you.

Now that you're spending so much time together and avoiding all the potential relationship pitfalls, you might be thinking, "Am I ready to move in with this guy?" Here's how you know if you're ready to start packing those moving boxes.

- **You spend most nights together already:** It would be a big jump to go from spending one night a week together to moving in. But if you're spending almost every night at his place anyway, then sometimes paying for two rents doesn't make sense, and one of you should consider moving in.
- **You're on the same page for the future:** Some couples don't ever want to get married. Some definitely do. Before you move in together, confirm a game plan for your relationship.
- **Money, money:** You've talked about who is going to pay for what. If he's moving into your place, are you going to split the rent fifty/fifty? What if you make more money than he does? How is that going to affect the bills? Nobody likes talking about money, but it's an important step before you move in.
- **You're ready to spend most nights *not* alone:** This part is hard. You have to be ready for the fact that almost every night, the person you live with is going to be around. Curling up in front of the TV and watching *Real Housewives* as you paint your nails is not going to be as easy when your man is around and wants to watch ESPN. Be prepared for what comes with sharing a space with someone: a lot of compromise.
- **You truly love each other:** Moving is so freaking hard. Only move in with a guy whom you're absolutely head over six-inch heels in love with.

And with these simple tips, you are going to have a healthy, successful relationship and live happily ever after.

# Afterword

"The thing about beginnings is there's magic in them. They're full of surprises and you never know what's going to happen. So here's to a lifetime of beginnings!"

Josh Kaminski, *Young & Hungry*

No matter how many things you learn from this book, you're always going to be growing, changing, and starting something new. This book is here for you as you throw your first dinner party, move into your first apartment, have your first relationship, get your first big job, roast your first chicken, and everything in between! And don't ever forget that you, like Gabi Diamond, are capable of doing anything. As she says in *Young & Hungry*, "The pie's the limit." So have a bite of that tasty hand pie you learned how to bake and get ready for the beginning of an exciting, flavorful, absolutely delicious life.